Fig. 1: Meditation posture—Full lotus.
圖1：靜坐姿勢——跏趺坐

Fig. 2: Full lotus 1—Subjugating posture
(with the left leg on top of the right).
圖2：全跏坐之一——降伏坐
（左腿押右腿）

Fig. 3: Full lotus 2—Auspicious posture
(with the right leg on top of the left).
圖3：全跏坐之二——吉祥坐
（右腿押左腿）

Fig. 6: Left half lotus posture.
圖6：左單跏坐

Fig. 5: Right half lotus posture.
圖5：右單跏坐

Fig. 4: Full lotus posture—Silhouette.
圖4：全跏坐側圖

A form in 'Tai-Chi Chuan: Left Grip on Sparrow's Tail
太極拳：左攬雀尾式

A form in 'Tai-Chi Chuan: Forward-step Push
太極拳：上步掤法式

Taken in front of the Shingon Hall at AB Temple
攝於美國遍照寺眞言殿

With American Students after their Taking Three Refuges
美國弟子皈依

The Dharma Banners Series 4

【法幢集4】習禪三部曲之一

A Trilogy of Ch'an — Part 1

禪 之 甘 露
The Sweet Dews of Ch'an

Lectures On Buddhism for English Meditation Class
at Chuang Yen Monastery, N.Y.

紐約莊嚴寺英語禪坐班講錄(1)

By Venerable Cheng Kuan
釋 成 觀 法 師 述著

新 逍 遙 園 譯 經 院
Neo-Carefree Garden Buddhist Canon Translation Institute

The Sweet Dews of Ch'an

Fourth edition
Copyright © 2005 by Vairocana Publishing Co., Ltd.
Second printing, 2007
Third printing, 2011 by Neo-Carefree Garden Buddhist Canon Translation Institute, A Charitable Trust Foundation
Fourth printing, 2015 by Neo-Carefree Garden Buddhist Canon Translation Institute
All Rights Reserved (**For free distribution only**)
Printed in Taiwan, R.O.C.

Third edition, Copyright © 2002 by Vairocana Publishing Co., Ltd., Taipei, Taiwan; this edition is a major revision of The Sweet Dews of Ch'an.
Second edition, Copyright © 1995 by Vairocana Publishing Co., Ltd., Taipei, Taiwan.
First edition, 1990 by Torch of Wisdom; 2nd print, 1996 by The Corporate Body of Buddha Educational Foundation, Taipei, Taiwan.

Distributing Centers:

1. Neo-Carefree Garden Buddhist Canon Translation Institute & Mahavairocana Temple

No. 15, Alley 6, Lane 4, Fu-Hsing Rd., Wenshan District
Taipei City 11691, Taiwan
Ph.: (02) 2934-7281   Fax: (02) 2930-1919
Website: www.abtemple.org

2. Americana Buddhist Temple

10515 N. Latson Rd., Howell, MI 48855, USA
Ph.: (517) 545-7559   Fax: (517) 545-7558
Website: www.abtemple.org

ISBN 957-9373-15-9

CONTENTS

DEDICATION

Namo Buddha, Namo Dharma, Namo Saṃgha.

May all the Multibeings

Have all their good wishes fulfilled

And attain the Supreme Bodhi

As soon as possible.

PREFACE
To the Third Revised Edition

This is a totally new edition of *The Sweet Dews of Ch'an*. In this edition, I have virtually revised every paragraph of the entire book, and in some pages, even every line of it, to the effect that it seems to me to be a "new" work. I have extensively revised and improved the diction, phraseology and Buddhist terms in the hope that it would greatly enhance the terminological and conceptual perspicuity, as well as the verbal fluency and readability. At the end of the book I also included a letter from a reader, as well as my response to it. This communication concerns the quality and status of Mahāyāna and Hinayāna, and the Buddhahood and the Arhathood. It could provide, I believe, poignant and interesting reading. Besides, since this is a totally new edition, I would suggest that the readers of previous editions also read this one; hopefully they would find out that the reading would be worth their while.

The Author.

On July 18, 2002, at AB Temple, Michigan

9

Chapter 1:

The Essentials of Ch'an Buddhist Meditation

Ch'an or *Zen* is the outcome of meditation. The purpose of meditation is usually not very well recognized; for different people have different ideas about the purpose of Ch'an: some people take it this way, while others would view it otherwise. But I am going to put it very simply and, when we go into the *Sūtra* (Buddhist Scripture), you will know more about the nature of *Ch'an*.

There are two "right" or "highest" purposes of *Ch'an*. The first purpose is to achieve *Dhyāna* (Sanskrit, **ध्या**). *Dhyāna* is a combination of relaxation, concentration and calmness or tranquility.

The second purpose of Ch'an is, using your very composed

1

and tranquil mind, to observe clearly all the *dharmas* or phenomena externally and internally. As an outcome of *Dhyāna*, you will be able to observe these phenomena very clearly because your "Mental Mirror" is very clear—for there are no more disturbances to veil it. Out of these observations will come Transcendental Wisdom, which in Sanskrit is called *Prajñā*.

What does this wisdom transcend? It enables us to transcend the Three Realms. (We will discuss this in detail later.) It enables us to transcend desire, attachment, anger, etc. so that we will not stay in *Samsara* or Transmigration any longer. We will be emancipated—emancipated, not through the mercy of anybody else, but rather through our own power of will and power of wisdom, coupled by the willingness to practice to achieve perfection. The total outcome will be *Dhyāna* plus *Prajñā* (ध ज्ञ): tranquility together with wisdom.

Therefore, tranquility is the "Body" of the power, and wisdom is the "Application" of this power. In the *Sūtra* the Buddha often instructs us, "to utilize the Sword of Wisdom to eliminate the Thieves of Worries and Troubles." Therefore *Dhyāna* plus *Prajñā* becomes *Samādhi* (स म ध). And *Samādhi*, in turn, is the tool that leads to Enlightenment.

There are diverse levels of Enlightenment; yet we should set our goal on the highest one, which is called *Anatana-samyak-sam bodhi*, or the Supreme Enlightenment. Although we should aim at the highest, and yet we should start from the lowest point in the execution. Probably just like Don Quixote, we are aiming at the presumably "impossible," with our head high in the air, and our feet treading solidly on the *terra firma*.

And so, the object that we are talking about here is the highest form of Buddhist meditation. More importantly, in meditation, we should not do it with a view to finding or looking for any "ghosts" or "devils." What is meant by ghosts or devils? When we sit in meditation, due to our past and present *Karmic Hindrances*, we might "see" or "hear" something out of the ordinary. Be it what it may, however, all those colors or sounds perceived are *delusive*, and cannot be counted on or trusted as real. You may do well just by ignoring them. Do not ever feel or think that those are your *credits* of practice. Although in some cases the phenomena in meditation may be good and real indeed, but if you become attached to any of them, they would be instantly transformed to be your stumbling stones in your overall practice. And just for that reason, very inconceivably bad things can happen to you in meditation pretty soon. Therefore, I need to inform and *warn* you at the very outset against these situations as a precaution for genuine High Meditation. You should look upon these phenomena as unfaithful "mistresses"—for sure you have to view them no other than that, and you should try to ignore them altogether and never become attached to them at all.

All the phenomena occurring in meditation, either mental or physical, can be good or bad; it totally depends on how you receive them. This is the fundamental rule of thumb that we need to develop and keep forever in mind: when anything comes up during meditation, do not be shocked, or taken aback. In some cases, during meditation, some people would "rock" their bodies or perspire profusely or become suddenly cold. They might envisage images beautiful or horrible. You should treat all of these as fleeting dreams. Do not be horrified by them, and do not engender a love toward them as some deluded people do, for that will lead you into deep trouble; specifically, the loving or apprehension of these phenomena could mislead one from misperception to a situation of bewilderment, or hallucination, or even to derangement and insanity. So you need to watch out for this!

These are the "Right Views" and essential starting points of meditation; we need to have these know-how beforehand in order to perform a good meditation, for we really have a long way to go in the way of Bodhi and so we cannot afford to be involved with mistakes like these.

Next, we need to be quite clear about the purpose of our practice by inquiring ourselves: "What are we trying to achieve in meditation?" Now let us try to answer this question. First of all, we are trying to calm our mind down and to eliminate Attachments, Aversions, and Ignorance that have been occupying our Mind. The Aversions, Anger, Jealousy, etc. are Defilements

to the Mind and they are called *karmas* (不对 in Sanskrit meaning "action"). These *Karmas* have been accumulating through
eons of ages. For they are formless and intangible; therefore,
without the Eye of Transcendental Wisdom, no one would be
able to perceive them, let alone eliminating them. Yet even if
we cannot perceive them with the naked eye, we still can vividly
feel their active presence, and unmistakably feel ourselves at
their mercy constantly.

Therefore, in meditation the first thing we must do is to
practice according to the correct rules. Since all games have
their own rules, and just because this "game" of Enlightenment
happens to be the most serious one, its rules are perforce the
most demanding of all. If we can but abide by these Rules, we
can be for sure to achieve excellent results. One of these excellent results would be to acquire the ability to "settle" all the
Defilements—just like settling the dregs in the muddy water of a
pond. Our mind is just like a Pond, which is full of muddy water
or Defilements. If we wish to wipe out the Defilements, we must
first of all try to "tranquilize" our mind, and not to agitate it in
any way. In order to quiet this mind of ours, we must sit in meditation and utilize a certain technique which is called *Śamatha*,
meaning the "Subjugation" or "Cessation" of worries. However,
Śamatha is not the final goal, since what it does is merely to
settle the Defilements like sediments to the bottom of the Mental
Pond—yet as "dregs" they still lie there; for *Śamatha* alone is

not capable of cleansing and eliminating the Mental Dregs.   In other words, after the genuine execution and accomplishment of *Śamatha*, on the surface level of the mind, it might look calm enough, but at the subconscious depth of the mind, the Defilements are still deposited quietly there.

The next step in meditation is to actually eliminate the deep-sunken Deposits of Karmic Defilements through *Vipaśyanā* (ཨིཔཤྱ་ན), or Transcendental Visualization. In order to perform *Vipaśyanā* well, we will need to acquire some Transcendental Wisdom first, because without this wisdom we would not be able to tackle our task. And so to review the whole process, the complete scenario of Meditation is that first of all we need to calm our perturbed mind down by means of *Śamatha*, so as to get the Karmic Defilements settled down to the bottom of our Mental Pond, and then secondly we can get rid of these Sediments for good by means of *Vipaśyanā* combined with *Śamatha*.

As for the ordinary beginner, the first principle of meditation is Relaxation; the second one is Concentration. Through concentration, you will develop the skill to attain *Prajñā* (Transcendental Wisdom). Since Transcendental Wisdom is not compatible with a wandering mind, you must first learn to harness your mind, and then to focus it on the contemplation of a certain Buddha *Dharma* so as to achieve *Śamatha*. Once you can get to *Śamatha*, you will be able to employ your mind like a "sword of wisdom" to cut through all entanglements of Vexations. And this is exactly the essential purpose of meditation.

Meditation, therefore, as we can see from the foregoing statement, does not mean merely to sit and seclude yourself from the crowd in order to achieve a few minutes of calmness or to enjoy some moments of quietude. That is only the very *first step*, not the ultimate goal. There is much more to meditation, and we will try to study all those things at large in this class as we go on.

The above are the fundamental concepts and principles about Buddhist meditation. Talking about specific techniques, for beginners, usually the first step is *Ānāpānasmṛti*, that is, the *breath-watching contemplation*. It involves watching your breaths and counting them from one to ten. In doing this meditation, you do not have to take deep breaths, though; just breathing naturally will do, for this is not any kind of physical exercise, but a mental one; nor is it *'chi kung*. As you inhale, you will count "one," and then exhale. As you inhale again, you will count "two." Do not count both the inhalations and the exhalations, only one or the other. If you should lose count, do not try to guess where you were and begin from that surmised point; rather, you should start from "one" all over again. After you have reached the number "ten," you will begin anew with number "one." Believe me, simple as it may sound, this is far from an easy task—Try it, and you will see what I am talking about. Anyhow, don't treat it lightly: If your mind is not clear and calm enough, you would just seem never to be able to reach number Ten.

When you sit, you must relax all of the muscles and bones and sinews in your body. Sit up straight, with your back bone up-right. Sit upon the front end of the meditation cushion; do not sit with the whole of your buttocks upon it. If you can sit in the full lotus position, by all means do so; if not, you should at least sit in the half-lotus position. Any other way of sitting will bring little and low meditational efficacy.

During sitting, relax your *body* first, and then try to relax your *mind*. Curl up the tip of your tongue to the alveolar ridge, or soft palate—this is very important. Close your mouth and breathe in and out through your nose only, and do it noiselessly; do not produce hissing or panting sound. Try to regulate your breathing as soft, smooth, and deep as naturally possible. The finer the breath is, the finer the mind will become; but you cannot force the breath to be fine abruptly—it comes only naturally through constant and painstaking practice.

In the practice of *Ānāpānasmṛti* when you can reach the point of concentrating your mind well, you can switch from the technique of "**Breath Counting**" to "**Breath Following**." By Breath Following it means to follow your inhaling Breath from your nostrils down through your throat, lungs, heart, and all the way to the whole of your body. At this time, try to view the air all over your body, your skin, and all the pores of your entire body. With this done well, then you can do the next technique of **"Cool-Warm Contemplation"**: that is, to feel the coolness of the air as it comes through your nostrils, and the warmth of it as it exits through your nostrils. After this, comes the **"Long-Short Contemplation."** In this contemplation the work is to observe whether each of your breath is long or short: sometimes the inhaling is long; at times it is shorter. Be fully aware of every aspect about your breathing—the most fundamental and vital phenomenon of your Life. When you can do this well, sometimes you can even feel the "sweetness" of the air at the tip of your tongue! (But do not anticipate it, though. If it happens, it is a good thing; if it does not, that's OK—after all, meditation is for the "transformation" of the *mind*, not of the *matter*.)

The striking of my Dharmic Instrument "Wood Fish" twice is the signal for the beginning of a meditation session. One strike on the small bell signals the end of the meditation session.

When the meditation session is finished, open up your eyes, rub your hands gently to warm them. Then, rub your eyes, face, and arms gently to restore them to normal circulation of the blood. Rub your legs gently before moving them or standing up.

Following the Sitting Meditation, we will practice some Walking Meditation. We will walk to the sound of the Wood Fish. As the striking becomes quicker and quicker, we will walk faster and faster until we gradually work into the Running Meditation. As you walk, you can repeat in your heart the phrase "Namo Ami-To Fo"—("Pay homage to Amitabha Buddha").

I have heard people say that most Western people are very fond of meditation; but to my amazement, many of them do not know that in order to practice meditation correctly they also need to acquire knowledge by reading the *Sūtras*, or Scriptures, for acquiring *knowledge* by reading the *Sūtras* is indispensable; otherwise, we will not have the proper, unmistakable, authentic techniques to guide us. Moreover, it is not just techniques, but the overall knowledge gained from them that will throw light into our lives, into the very deepest niche of our hearts.

As there are numerous helpful methods in meditation, what I am going to do is to give you a comprehensive presentation of these methods accompanied by a little practice on each of them. In this way you will have an overall idea about meditation techniques, which will help you to select one of them that can best suit you. The Buddha related an illustrious parable in one of his greatest *Sūtras*, *The Sūtra of Mahā-Paranirvāṇa*: Some people who were born blind were touching an elephant in order to find out what an elephant looked like. One blind man touched the trunk and thought that an elephant looked like a long tube. Another blind man touching its tail imagined that an elephant was like a rope. Each of these blind men touching different parts of the animal had his own concept of the elephant's looks. They were all telling the truth as they "perceived," and *they were all right*—yet *they were all wrong*. They were only telling part of the whole Truth. Thus, there is a danger in presenting only part of the facts. However, there is also a jeopardy in presenting everything altogether; for in that way, you *may* think that *you know everything*, and take *Knowing* for *practice*. Although you might seem to know everything, without actual practice, it will not do you any good; therefore, you won't be able to enjoy the fruit of practice.

And so my approach will be to help you get the whole picture of Meditation, and then we will practice as many methods as we can. Finally, we will stick to only one or two of these methods to the end and practice on them strenuously. Then hopefully we will accomplish something! This is my view about meditation learning and I will try to do it this way. In the meantime, this approach was also the method most adopted by great masters in the past.

—Lecture given on 9/17/1988

Chapter 2:

Some Basic Concepts and Terms about Meditation

In order to do meditation effectively in a professional way, we need to acquaint ourselves with some basic terms and concepts at the outset.

Relaxation and Concentration

Relaxation and Concentration are the two most basic techniques in meditation. Since our Mind is always disturbed by anxiety, we need to tame and quiet it down by getting it to the opposite side, i.e., Relaxation. Moreover, because our mind is constantly wandering at large, we need to "harness" it by the "bridle" of concentration, so that our energy is not squandered or misused in useless thinking or action.

The Six Dusts (Guṇas)

The Six *Guṇas* (**ऽ ॓** or "Dusts") are the objects that "feed" the Six Senses: Form, Sound, Smell, Flavor, Touch, and Concept. So these Six *Guṇas* are like food to the Six Senses: in a way of speaking, the Six Senses live on the Six *Guṇas*; by the acquisition of the Six *Guṇas*, the Six Senses can live and grow. The Six *Guṇas* are called "Dusts" for they can obscure the vision of our Inner Mind or Buddha Nature.

The Six Senses

The Six Senses are the Six Sensory Organs (eye, ear, nose, tongue, body and mind) that react to and grasp the Six Dusts respectively: i.e. the Eye grasps the Visual Dust; the Ear grasps the Auditorial Dust; the Nose grasps the Smelling Dust; the Tongue grasps the Taste Dust; the Body grasps the Tactile Dust; the Mind grasp the Dharmic Dust.

The Eight Cognizances (Vijñānas)

Cognizance (or *Vijñāna* (व ज्ञ न)) means the capability or functioning of recognition and comprehension. This is by and large the most significant and profound word in Buddhist Doctrine. Specifically, the Eight Cognizances are the eight levels or components of our Mind. The first five levels, also called The First Five Cognizances, arise as a result of the interaction between the Five Dusts with the Five Senses. These Cogni-zances when they come into being they do not carry any interpretations about the Dusts—they are, in another word, crude perceptions or rudimentary recognitions.

And then when the Sixth Cognizance comes into play, all kinds of feelings, opinions, and judgments will be formed. Therefore, the Sixth Cognizance is the one that does all the differentiating.

The Seventh Cognizance is the Center of Ego, for all our Egoistic opinions, Attachments, and adherences are the working of this Cognizance.

The Eighth Cognizance is the *Ālaya* (or *Ālayagarbha*), "the Repertorial Cognizance," or the storehouse of all *karmas*, whether they be good, bad, or neutral—all the karmas done are collected and accumulated in this Cognizance, which is the Main Body (or Corpus) of the Psyche (or the Mind).

Dhyāna

Dhyāna (𑀣𑁆𑀬𑀸𑀦) is often used as a general term for "meditation," or as the outcome of quietude or tranquility gained through meditation. It can also mean the middle way between *Śamatha* and *Vipaśyanā*. The first effect that *Dhyānaic* meditation gains is the ability to clarify our "Mental Water" of the Six Dusts so as to reduce their influence on the emotions, sensory impressions, and thoughts in our mind. This efficacy of *Dhyāna* will gradually enable us to liberate ourselves from the disturbances of external stimuli.

Śamatha

Śamatha (𑀰𑀫𑀣) means the quietude achieved through the practice of *dhyāna*. It serves as the springboard for starting to learn the Buddhist Teachings. *Śamatha*, by itself, is not of immense value unless we utilize it as a powerful tool to strive for Enlightenment.

Vipaśyanā

Vipaśyanā (𑀯𑀺𑀧𑀰𑁆𑀬𑀦) means the Visualizations performed in meditation, especially those done after one has achieved

Śamatha. When in *Śamathic* quietude, in order to develop Transcendental Wisdom, one will need to practice the techniques of various Buddhist Visualizations, such as the Four Contemplations, the Contemplations Upon Physical Uncleanliness, etc.

Samādhi

Samādi (𑖭𑖦𑖯𑖠𑖰), or Equanimity, is the perfectly balanced effect of both *Śamatha* and *Vipaśyanā*. If there is too much *Śamatha* in meditation, the mind will tend to be too still to the point of dullness or dormancy; while too much *Vipaśyanā* will incline to make the mind too elevated and excited, or even restless. Only the balanced state of *Samādi* can keep the mind at once calm and keen with perceptive wisdom.

Prajñā

Prajñā (𑖢𑖿𑖨𑖕𑖿𑖗𑖯), or Transcendental Wisdom, is the consummate fruition gained through proficient *Samādhi*, i.e., the perfectly balanced combination of *Śamatha* (quietude) with *Vipaśyanā* (Visualization) as stated above. This Transcendental Wisdom is the eventual outcome of all the practices on Buddhism. And it is the power of this *Prajñāic Wisdom* that actually enables the practitioner to see through his Timeless Nescience (or Ignorance) and break it apart, and thereby to perceive and realize in full his Buddha Nature and become fully enlightened. Therefore the great *Prajñāic Wisdom* is actually the final goal that a Buddhist practitioner aims at, for without it, any Enlightenment would be impossible. But again, *Prajñāic Wisdom* does not stand alone: it comes from long-term innumerable painstaking strenuous practice on all aspects of the Dharmas. It does not come easy; nor is it of a sudden flash of inspiration or "revelation," or anything like that.

—Lecture given on 8/20/1988

Chapter 3:

Some Advanced Meditation Techniques

Here are some other advanced *Vipaśyanic* meditation techniques, which are very significant in Buddhist meditation practice.

A. The Four Contemplations

The Four Contemplations are designed to meditate upon the Body, the Feelings, the Mind, and the Dharma. In doing this meditation, generally, we are to contemplate *the physical Body as Defiled, the Sensations as Afflicting, the Mind as Transient,* and *the Dharmas as Egoless.* However, we can also make a lot of variations and combinations, such as to view the *Body* as either *Defiled*, or *Afflicting*, or *Transient*, or *Egoless* respectively, or all four of them at the same time. That is to say that after some time of practice, when we become fairly good at the individual items, we can also try at combining some or all the items together and do it at the same time. For instance, we can view the Body at the same time as *Defiled* and *Afflicting*; or as *Defiled*, *Afflicting*, and *Transient*; or as *Defiled*, *Afflicting*, *Transient*, and *Egoless*. After having practiced these well, we can also move on to *Sensation* and do the same combinational Visualizations on it. With *Sensation* done well, we can then proceed to do the same with the *Mind* and the *Dharma* as well. The combinational Visualizations can be shown in the following chart thus:

Meditate upon the   **In relation to**

I. Body

- Defiled
- Afflicting
- Transient
- Egoless

2. Sensations

- Afflicting
- Defiled
- Transient
- Egoless

3. Mind

- Transient
- Defiled
- Afflicting
- Egoless

4. Dharma

- Egoless
- Defiled
- Afflicting
- Transient

a) The Body is Defiled

"*Body*" here stands for the eye, the ear, the nose, the tongue and the skin, whereas "Defilement" can mean either material or spiritual or metaphysical uncleanliness. On the one hand, the reason why the Body is called unclean is owing to the excretions of the five organs. This is the material uncleanliness. On the metaphysical side, the Body is viewed as unclean is due to the fact that the sense organs delight in grasping things that are harmful for us (i.e., the "Dusts"), which would obstruct us in practice or keep us from getting to the final goal of Enlightenment.

b) The Sensations are Afflicting

There are three kinds of *Sensations*: Pleasure, Pain, and Neutral Ones. In respect of sensations, the primal doctrine is that all Sensations are painful, for all sensations are impermanent, transient, ungraspable, and as a result, they turn out to be unreal, illusive and deceptive. All Sensations that we grasp or procure would bring to us, in the end, more pains than pleasure. It is on this account that Sensations are regarded as Afflicting.

c) The Mind is Transient

The *Mind* is transient or inconstant in that it really does not have any Real Entity to itself. What it does have is merely the "shadows" or images grasped from the interactions between the Five Sense Organs and the Five Dusts; therefore, these shadows are exactly like the images shown on a movie screen—although actually the movies are "unreal," they still vividly appear on the screen, with colors, shapes, sounds, even imaginable tastes and smells; and there are also hate and love, war and peace, heaven and hell lively manifested on the screen. Nevertheless, the movie screen is still ultimately *blank* and *uncontaminated* as ever. Such is also the same with the images on our Mental Screen: no matter how crowdedly the Mental Screen is filled with detrimental images, the Mental Screen itself always remains ultimately blank and clean without any contaminating stains. Besides, the mind of an ordinary person is exactly like a Monkey, or like the Wind, or Lightning, or a drop of Morning Dew—for the Monkeyish Mind never sits still, it never dwells a long time; it changes from second to second. This is the way to do the contemplation on the Mind as Transient.

d) The Dharma is Egoless

The word *Dharma* (𑀥𑀭) originally means "law" in Sanskrit. In Buddhism it has two meanings:

1. Everything in the world is called a *dharma*, either physical or mental or spiritual, animated or inanimated, formative or formless, tangible or intangible, since everything in the world has all got a law to its own; therefore, each thing is called a *dharma*.

2. Buddha's Teaching is called *Buddha Dharma*, or sometimes simply *Dharma* in brief. For it goes without saying that the Buddha's Teaching, like all *dharmas*, has its own laws to follow; consequently, it has come to be called *Dharma* as well.

However, the "Dharma" here in the Four Contemplations refers to the first kind of dharma, meaning everything in general. As for the word "Ego" here it signifies something having an Entity that can act fully independent of anything else. But we know that anything in this world cannot be totally divorced from other things. All the worldly things are *dependent* upon each other to function, or so as to survive. They are just like a bundle of reeds, if separated, none of them can stand upright and survive. This state of *interdependence* (or mutual reliance) of all things is called *Egolessness* by the Buddha. And all *dharmas*, in the final analysis, are in this kind of *interdependent existence*; therefore, they can not be totally do without others—they are not totally "free" to act on its own, or at its own will alone. And so it follows that no *dharma* has a real *Ego* to itself. This is one way to do the contemplation on the *dharmas* as Egoless.

B. The Contemplations on the Four Elements—Earth, Water, Fire, Air

One of the techniques in meditating on the Four Elements involves visualizing everything as being of *the same color*. If everything were of the same "color," then everything would look plain and unattractive, and as a result, we will begin to lose preferences and Attachments for things. And eventually, all judgments will be discarded and *the Wisdom of Ultimate Equality* can be attained.

Another way to meditate upon the Four Elements is to contemplate that all four of them, as well as each one of them, are *Transient, Afflicting, Vacuous, and Egoless*, very much the same way as we contemplated upon Forms before. Besides, because the outstanding nature of the Four Elements is *impermanent* and *transient*, we can thereby arrive at a conclusion that the Four Elements are *Egoless*, for in these Elements there is not an unchanged Entity in any one of them for us to hold on to and claim: "This *is* the Matter!" Therefore, their nature is all *egoless* and *vacuous*, and for this reason they are afflicting to us, because we cannot have any sure grip on either of them, in terms of comprehension or possession. Having so contemplated well, we will neither cling to the *Inner Four Elements* (i.e., our body), nor be attached to the *Outer Four Elements* (i.e., the world) so much as we used to, and thereby will be *liberated* from the entanglement of Matter soon.

C. The Contemplation on the Mind

Besides the contemplation on Buddha Nature, this is by far the most profound meditation of all, since the Mind is without shape and form, and it is more like abstract thing and can only be seen or imagined with the *Mental Eye*, or *the Eye of Wisdom*. The Mind is so fleeting that it is extremely difficult for one to observe. If only we can be *aware* of our Mind *at all times*, we will not go wrong with anything, nor will we commit or speak anything detrimental to ourselves or others. ***"Those who are able to observe their mind will be liberated; those who are unable to observe their mind will forever be under bondage,"*** says the Buddha in a *Sūtra* (*The Sūtra of the Buddha's Past Lives and the Visualization of the Mental Ground*). Please contemplate on this Sacred Dictum.

D. The Contemplation on the Buddha Nature

The Buddha Nature is also called the *Original Nature*. Let me make use of an analogy of a *gold mine* to illustrate the meaning of this term. The Buddha is the person that has excavated and refined the gold of his own *Original Nature*. We, ordinary as we now are, also have the same quality and quantity of gold in our mental mine as the Buddha; the only difference is that we have not yet dug it out and got it purified. Therefore, *although we have the same amount and quality of treasure as the Buddha does, we still live in poverty without any merit since we have not been aware of our Buddha Nature and actually worked to acquire it yet!*

To contemplate upon this analogy, and to view all phenomena as the manifestations of our Buddha Nature, will deepen and broaden our wisdom and quicken our pace toward Enlightenment.

—Lecture given on 8/27/1988

Chapter 4:

The "Five Flavors" of Ch'an

（五味禪）

A. A Prelude:
The Composition of the Mind

In Sanskrit, *Dhyāna*, as I said before, means *Ch'an* or *Zen*. (*Zen* is the Japanese pronunciation for the same Chinese word 禪 or *Ch'an*.) There are five categories of Ch'an called the "Five Flavors" of Ch'an.

In order to make it clear to you what I am going to enunciate about the Five Flavors of Ch'an, at the outset, I would like to present to you the Buddhist theory about the Mind and the Cognizances. *Cognizance* means the Mind's ability or function of recognizing or comprehending both external and internal things, or more importantly, the Mind itself. According to the Buddha, there are Eight Levels of recognizing ability of the Mind called the *Eight Cognizances*, and each of them stands for one kind of recognizing function.

The First Five Cognizances

The upper level of the Mind consists of **the First Five Cognizances**. These cognizances come into being as the result of the interaction between the Five Senses (eye, ear, nose, tongue, and body) and the "Five Dusts" (form, sound, smell, flavor, and touch). The First Five Cognizances do not do any subtle differentiating work, for their functioning is of the crudest or rudimentary recognition; in other words, they are not "opinionated" in any way.

The Sixth Cognizance

The second level of the Mind is **the Sixth Cognizance**—it is this Cognizance that conducts all the sophisticated *Differentiatings*. Consequently, this becomes the Judgemental and Discriminating office of our Mind. It ponders, weighs and discriminates upon the images of the Five Dusts collected by the Five Senses. This level of our Mind tends to consider itself as the "boss";

An Analytic Chart of the Mind

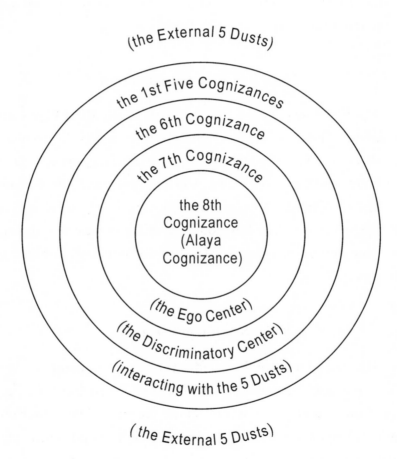

(the External 5 Dusts)

the 1st Five Cognizances

the 6th Cognizance

the 7th Cognizance

the 8th
Cognizance
(Alaya
Cognizance)

(the Ego Center)

(the Discriminatory Center)

(interacting with the 5 Dusts)

(the External 5 Dusts)

that is, it looks upon itself to some degree as "in control" of the affair. But, as a matter of fact, it still needs to take orders from someone else—the Seventh Cognizance, which is very much like the hidden "boss" of the Sixth Cognizance. What is more, the Sixth Cognizance usually tries very hard to rationalize and make all sorts of justifications for this hidden Director. Therefore, the Sixth Cognizance is somewhat like a foreman or middleman in that it stands in between the First Five and the Seventh Cognizances.

The Seventh Cognizance

The third level of our Mind is **the Seventh Cognizance**, also called the Ego Center. For this Cognizance incessantly grasps the Eighth Cognizance as ME and in the meantime deems the First Six Cognizances as MINE, and thereby constructs the Ego Center. This Cognizance is also the level which clandestinely determines how the First Six Cognizances should act or react to the external world—i.e. they all secretly do its biddings. Nevertheless, the ordinary people would not be able to perceive this Ego, because it has itself all covered up behind all sorts of rationalizations and subterfuges which are consciously or unconsciously manufactured and furnished by "the foreman," the Sixth Cognizance.

The Eighth Cognizance

The fourth level of the Mind under the Ego Center is **the Eighth Cognizance**, also called *Ālaya* Cognizance ("Ālaya" meaning storage). This is the storage house or database of all the cognizances, the jumbo repertory for all the Karmas done by the Seven Cognizances. And so the Eighth Cognizance is, to put it in another way, the *Psyche* for all Multibeings (or Mortal Beings).

The First Five Cognizances together with the Sixth one enable us to function, or take actions in our daily life. Generally speaking, those daily actions of ours, if repeated for several times, will form themselves into habits and are thereby pressed down into the Seventh and Eighth Cognizance. Once they reach the Eighth Cognizance, they can resurface during a time we least expect them to and in such a way that can startle us. And those same unexpected resurfacing things are sometimes mysteriously called as "inspirations."

In certain situations, the data stored in the Eighth Cognizance will emerge. Incidents like this do not only occur in our waking hours, but also in our dreams—and so far as Freud is concerned, it does more so in our dreams.

Habits are at once a blessing and a curse to us—a blessing, because without them life is almost impossible; if we would have to think about literally everything before we do it, we would be in tremendous hardships. And thanks to the existence of Habits, we do not have to think or deliberate for each action we take. But Habit is also a curse, for they can enslave us. [Example of how the habit of smoking is brought down into the Seventh and Eighth Cognizances and becomes a "habit" is given by the Reverend through "enacting" at this point.]

Everything we do is called *Karmas*, or actions. There are three kinds of *Karmas*: Physical Karma, Verbal Karma, and Mental Karma. In our conscious mind, when our deliberate actions are done, they are pressed down to the unseen levels beneath to be stored and made ready for use later on, just like ready-made suits or a drive-through hamburger restaurant, to the effect that we really do not need to think about what we are doing anymore; we just act through these habits. In other words, on a larger scale, we have been *carried along* by our previous *Karmas*, which are so abstruse that they are far beyond our imagination or thinking, and in a given situation they will just spring into view in an almost inexplicable manner. That is why people would at some time or other feel a strong drive to do something that they never know why they wanted to do it so much at all. Well, it is just the unconscious pushing force from previous *Karmic Habits*. Karmic Habitual Force is a blind force, totally unrecognizable and inconceivable to the ordinary people.

Now, let us see how the workings of the Eight Cognizances are related to the "Five Flavors" of Ch'an.

B. The Five Flavors of Ch'an

The interrelationships between the five kinds of Ch'an and the eight Cognizances will be discussed in each section below respectively.

1. The Worldly Meditation

This kind of Ch'an or meditation is practiced by mundane people who wish to improve their physical well-being or health and in some cases, wish to achieve some extraordinary states of experience. For instance, some of them would try to employ the power derived from their meditation to be able to stop their heartbeat or pulse temporarily, or to levitate or suspend their body in the air, or to be squeezed into a tiny box, or to be buried alive in a tomb or under water for a duration of time, etc. It is beyond a doubt that some of these people are able to achieve the state of concentration similar to *Śamatha*, by which they can suspend their breath or manifest some *tour de force*. Nevertheless, such execution of extraordinary feats, at its best, are nothing but physical stunts. Feats or stunts, however breath-taking they might appear, can never result in any Wisdom, not to speak of Enlightenment. Nor can they clarify or quiet one's Mind. In fine, they cannot enable you to benefit either yourself or others by increasing a gossamer of Wisdom.

The execution of this kind of Worldly Meditation is based upon the Five Senses. The Five Senses, in turn, will give birth to the First Five Cognizances in our Mind after contact with the Five Dusts. The Five Senses are physical; whereas the Five Cognizances are mental. The Five Senses would grasp or appropriate the Five Dusts (form, sound, smell, flavor, and touch). These external matters are called "Dusts" because they can veil up or becloud our Mind—specifically, they can blind our Mental Eye. Usually, the Five Senses would grasp a variety of images of the Dusts into the Mind, to ruminate upon them, and to relish and cherish both the Dusty shadows and the whole procedures. Thus the Worldly Meditation is carried out through the employment of the Five Senses and the Five Dusts, so as to result in some sensational consequences on the Fist Five Cognizances. Therefore, its accomplishment is unavoidably quite rudimentary and superficial; and as such, they are not to be taken seriously by the wise.

2. Other Religions' Meditation

In some other religions they practice meditation, too. But according to the Buddha, their practices are by and large based upon some faulty views or beliefs and, therefore, more often than not, they go astray from the Right Path. Their fault lies in that, according to the Buddha, instead of *seeking from within* themselves, some of them would **seek from outside** for something that can save them from their sins or faults, while others would seek illusively *to unite themselves with some external thing, or Being,* or concept, claiming that in that way they are "returning to their Creator," which is only an imaginary myth.

The practice of this category of meditation is based upon the Five Senses and the Five Dusts, in association with The First Five Cognizances and a little work of the Sixth Cognizance. That is to say, this category of meditation is a little higher, or deeper, than the Worldly Meditation, due to its slim employment of the Sixth Cognizance. Nevertheless, it is still not a desirable form of meditation, for the Sixth Cognizance is based on secret decrees from the Ego Center, and so more often than not it would make delusive or faulty judgements. Therefore, this meditation is still not desirable for our pursuit.

After the Five Senses have taken the images or shadows of the Five Dusts into the Mind, the Mind will then go on to ponder upon these shadows like this: Are these things good or evil? desirable or undesirable? right or wrong?—and so on, and so forth. As a result of these ponderings or deliberations, almost at that same instant, the First Five Cognizances will usher the Sixth Cognizance into play. The Sixth Cognizance is contaminated for it is guided by the Ego Cognizance, the Seventh one, named *Manaḥ* Cognizance, upon whose injunctions the Sixth

Cognizance formulates all our judgements, opinions, and sense of values. In sum, Other Religions' Meditation does not go deep enough in that it reaches only the surface of the Sixth Cognizance; and also for this reason, other Religions' Meditation is, to a great extent, hampered and beguiled by both the Sixth and Seventh Cognizance through their own well-sounding rationalizations on faulty Deliberations and subconscious Egotism.

3. Minor-Vehicle Ch'an

The previous two kinds of meditation (the Worldly and Other Religions' Meditations) are also called the Mundane Meditations. (Incidentally, the fact that they are entitled as "Meditation," rather than Ch'an, is due to this author's discretion, not carelessness, so as to distinguish the right from the wrong. Besides, the word *Ch'an*, to the author, has a connotation of sacredness, authenticity, and legitimacy.) The reason why the Compassion of the Minor-Vehicle practitioners is limited is because they are not interested in generating the wish to deliver other Multibeings. Their aim is solely for their own Liberations. Once they can liberate themselves from *Samsara*, or Transmigration, they *are not going to* return to this inflicted and defiled world again. Therefore, their goal is confined by the Ego. Nor are they interested in attaining the Ultimate Enlightenment, for they would not aim at the highest accomplishment so as to benefit all Multibeings.

They feel content with *Arhathood*, because it is good enough to deliver themselves, even though it would be far insufficient for the emancipation of all Multibeings—it would take the great Compassion and Wisdom of Buddhahood to be able to undertake this enterprise. (Undoubtedly it is much easier to help only oneself without having to bother about other people's difficulties.) And so you can see that the quest of Buddhahood is such an immensely hard and long enterprise!

The practice of the Minor-Vehicle Ch'an is generally based upon the Annihilation or total suppression of the First Six Cognizances—which the *Hinayāna* practitioners call *Nirvāṇa*. As a matter of fact, the *Hinayānic Nirvāṇa* is brought about by the willful suppression of the First Six Cognizances to the extent that their Six Cognizances would remain dormant or seemingly expired. This is far from a desirable way of practice for *Bodhisattvahood* practitioners, for it would enable one, as it were, to indulge oneself in self-obsessed quietude, while neglecting all the needs and pains of other Multibeings who are fighting and groping their way toward Liberation and *Bodhi*.

4. Major-Vehicle Ch'an (Bodhisattvic Ch'an)

Contrasted with the Minor-Vehiclists, the Bodhisattvic Ch'an cultivators would not simply concentrate upon their own Liberation. When they are able to solve their own problems to a great extent, they would then go a step further to try to help benefit others by the wisdom they have acquired.

The practice of this category of Ch'an is based upon the Elimination of the Seventh Cognizance as well as some primal Cultivation on the Eighth Cognizance. The Elimination of the Seventh Cognizance, the Ego Center, would enable these practitioners to engage themselves in altruistic endeavors without considering their own interests or benefits. And they would be able to ignore the trouble and hardship involved in benefiting others. Besides, the initial Cultivation on the Eighth Cognizance would promote the *Bodhisattvic* Ch'an practitioner's wisdom to such a level as closer to Buddhahood.

5. The Tathāgata Ch'an (The Buddha's Ch'an)

Tathāgata (རྷ) is a Meritorious Epithet for the Buddha, meaning "Thusness" or "Thus-Adventist." The Chinese version of this word is "Ru-Lai." *Tathāgata Ch'an* (or "*Ru-Lai Ch'an*") is also called "Patriarchic Ch'an" since it was handed down from the Buddha to the First Patriarch, Mahākāśyapa, and from him to later patriarchs. Hence, it is the highest form of Ch'an.

The central practice of this Ch'an deals mainly with the Eighth Cognizance and yet to a much more profound degree than the previous categories—so profound is this Ch'an that it is almost inconceivable to ordinary people.

The fulfillment of *Ru-Lai Ch'an* would result in the complete awareness as well as the ultimate *Transformation* of all Defilements into Merits, of all Ignorance into *Prajñā*, and of all the Three Venoms (Attachment, Aversion, and Ignorance) into the "Three Non-Leaking Virtues," (Precepts, *Samādhi*, and Wisdom.) The total outcome achieved in this Ch'an is, in one word, *the witnessing of one's Buddha Nature.* However, it should be noted that at this level of Ch'an, the work is done not through *Elimination,* but through *Transformation;* because at this level the Wisdom has become so powerful that it can *transform* everything and turn everything into good use: nothing at all is useless, and nothing will be wasted. Such is the Transcendental Power of Buddha *Tathāgata's* Ch'an!

The key to the accomplishment of Ru-Lai Ch'an, in fine, is Non-reliance: In performing the Ru-Lai Ch'an, one is not going to rely on anything whatsoever—forms, shapes, colors, breath, or even *Dharma*, anything at all. In this Non-reliant way you are to execute your *Tathāgatha Ch'an*, which would mean as much as to say: "Ascend to the Heavens, but you should do it without using a ladder or a rope, without taking an airplane, and even without jumping. All you are required to do is just Ascending unreliantly." This sounds very much like a "Kong-An"; yet it *is* a *Kong-An*—as a matter of fact, it is by far the toughest one! (Incidentally, there is another *Kong-An* in the similar vein; it goes like this: "Speak—without opening your mouth!") Such is the inconceivability in the *Tathāgata Ch'an*, which is the highest execution in the field of Meditation and *Prajñā*.

—Lecture given on 9/17/1988

Chapter 5:

The "Five Contemplations for Ceasing the Perturbed Mind"
（五停心觀）

I wish to introduce to you, the "Five Contemplations for Ceasing the Perturbed Mind." This also comes under the head of the third stage of the "Six Wondrous Dharmic Portals," which is called *Śamatha*, or "Cessation."

When our mind is troubled or perturbed, it is difficult to calm or still it. The Mind is without a form; it is invisible and ungraspable; therefore, we are almost helpless when we try to calm it down. Thanks to the Buddha's wisdom, numerous ingenious ways have been revealed to us in order to accomplish this task.

Although there can be thousands of means to still the mind, their chief essence can be grouped under five major types, which are called the Five Contemplations for Ceasing the Perturbed Mind:

(1) Ānāpānasmṛti—for destroying Wandering thinkings.

(2) The Contemplation on Uncleanliness—for destroying Attachments or Avarice.

(3) The Contemplation on the "Twelve Causality Links"—for destroying Ignorance.

(4) The Contemplation on Compassion—for destroying Aversions and Hate.

(5) The Contemplation on Buddha's Merits—for destroying Heavy Black Karmas.

Each of these meditations respectively consists of several levels, which are the rudimentary, the intermediate, the advanced, and the profound level. It depends on your skill, knowledge and comprehension to decide on which level of the contemplation you can undertake.

(1) Ānāpānasmṛti
(Contemplation on the Breath)

In Sanskrit, *Nāpāna* means breathing or breathing in; *Ā* is a prefix, meaning the opposite of something. *Ānāpāna*, therefore, means breathing in and out, and *Smṛti* means to watch. And so the whole word comes to mean "watching the breath coming in and out."

The direct purpose of this meditation is to remind us *to come back to our own person*; that is, to *search inward* rather than *outward*. The inner self, however, is so deep and profound that it is very hard for ordinary people to reach. The Buddha, therefore, has bestowed upon us this method of Breathwatching. The first step of this contemplation, Breath Counting, is comparatively easier than some other kinds, since everyone, no matter how rich or poor, must breathe; therefore, this method is open to all. In other words, it is *easily accessible* and *readily affordable* —it costs you nothing to do it. It also **helps you to come back to yourself**, and **to realize that you are living because you breathe**: in practicing this meditation you might for the first time in your life become aware of the fact that you are breathing!

The goal of this meditation is to **stop the wandering mind** in order to **attain concentration**. Our mind tends to wander from moment to moment and become highly uncontrollable. By practicing this meditation we can *discipline our mind to stay at one single point* for quite a long time. At the outset, we may be able to stay on that point (such as the Breath, or the act of breathing, or the counting of the numbers) for probably only a few seconds before our mind begins to wander away again. This is the crucial point—once we are aware that our mind has wandered away from the point of concentration, we should bring ourselves back to our concentration. Consequently, this meditation becomes not just the practice on Concentration, but also the practice of

Mindfulness or Awareness. You should try to stay aware at all times—that is, to stay at "home!" Do not run astray after External Objects. Each time our mind wanders away, we need to pull it back again by force, if necessary. We need to do this over and over again, until we can destroy the *Habit of Wandering*. Bad habits, however, are difficult to quit; that is why we must persevere steadfastly with this practice until we become very good at concentrating our Mind. This is the essential of *Ānāpānasmṛti*.

(2) The Contemplation on Uncleanliness

There are two kinds of "Uncleanliness": the physical uncleanliness and the mental uncleanliness. According to the Buddha, we are "inverted" in most of our views. Just like flies, we look upon all the worldly defiled objects as desirable and palatable, and we are so attached to these Defilements that we cannot give them up. In order to cure ourselves of this "perversion," we need to practice this meditation as a "correcting" means.

Therefore, this meditation is designed to help us get rid of Attachments, which is one of the most difficult tasks that we need to undertake. I will make a more detailed presentation on this contemplation later, right after this general account of the Five Contemplations.

(3) The Contemplation on the Twelve Causality Links

This meditation is a great subject in Buddhist Teaching, for it involves one of the most significant doctrines set forth by the Buddhas: the Doctrine of "**Cause and Effect**." This doctrine is very important in the Cultivation of wisdom. If we wish to know what "cause and effect" or "Karmic Causality" really is, then we definitely need to acquire the knowledge about this meditation. Moreover, we would also need to comprehend this meditation in great detail, not just the terminology itself, but the working of the whole system.

The ultimate goal of this meditation is to eliminate or cease Nescience or Ignorance (*Avidia* in Sanskrit, meaning Lightlessness or Benightedness). By Ignorance, the Buddha means to be ignorant of the true causes and effects, of how things come to be in their present state, and how they are destroyed and reborn. In one word, Nescience means the ignorance of the actual state of things or beings. There are twelve causes and effects, of which the First Link is *Nescience*.

Due to the blind force of Nescience, the mind of the Multibeing is moved or motivated into action, which results in Kinesis, or Motion and Working. This *Kinesis* becomes the Second Link. If the mind is motivated, it will be able to move everything else. So, everything else comes into being or changes due to that Primal Blind Motion. In the wake of this Motion, *Cognizance* arises. This Cognizance, as the Third Link, however, is not the ultimate consciousness of the Original Nature. It is rather the "False Consciousness" (or the Faulty Mind), which embodies the Initial wrong views, faulty Differentiation or Discrimination. Owing to Faulty Cognizance, there arises *Form and Name*. This is the Fourth Link.

"Form" stands for the physical and so it is visible; while "Name" refers to the mental and therefore invisible. The visible and the invisible combine themselves together to form everything else. Form and Name causes the genesis of the *Six Roots* or *Six Senses*, which becomes the Fifth Link.

When the Six Senses come into contact with both the internal and the external phenomena, the Sixth Link of *Contact* arises from it.

After the arising of Contact, *Perception* or *Sensation*, the Seventh Link, is brought forth.

Sensation is very crucial to Multibeings, for happiness, unhappiness, anger, love, etc., are all products of Sensations. We take Sensations or our feelings so seriously that we can never tolerate to have our feelings hurt. Whenever there is Sensation or Perception, *Attachment,* the Eighth Link will arise.

We tend to look upon our Sensations not just as our attitudes toward some objects, but rather as *a part of ourselves*: thus my feelings are virtually ME or MINE. Therefore, it is very difficult to detach ourselves from Sensation. Specifically, the hardest part for us to disassociate from is not the physical matter, but our mental feelings derived from it. If there is Attachment, then *Appropriation* or *Grasping,* the Ninth Link, arises.

Generally, we hold on to our feelings very strongly, and when we grasp them, we claim that we "own" these feelings. Therefore people usually say: I "have" anger in my mind—I "have" it; I "own" it; it is mine. In this sense, the anger is *owned* by you as if it were a piece of property. Furthermore, if you do own some property, there is no way that you would let go of it easily. Hence, after Grasping, *Owning* or *Possessiveness*, which is the Tenth Link, will come into being. Subsequent to Possessiveness, there will arise *Genesis* or *Birth,* the Eleventh Link, which will in turn lead to the Twelfth Link: *Senility, Illness,* and *Demise* or *Death* and all other *Afflictions.* Therefore, all these put together are called "one large agglomeration of afflictions," in the *Sūtra.*

After death, there will be **Rebirth** or **Reincarnation**. Thus, all of these links form a cycle, called **the Cycle of the Twelve Causality Links**. These twelve elements are fused together like a chain. They go round and round without ending. Each one of them can be at once a Cause of that which follows after it and an Effect of that which precedes it. It is such an unending circle that without the "Sword of *Prajñā*" (Transcendental Wisdom),

The Cycle of the Twelve Causality Links

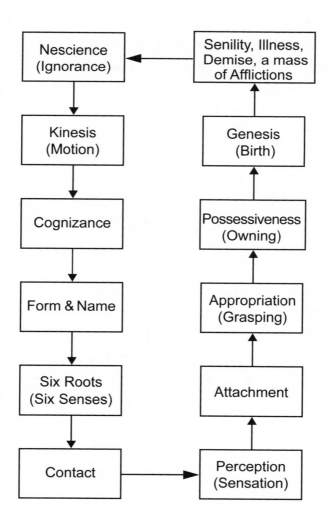

there is no way to break off the bondage of this chain. As for Worldly wisdom, it is even not sufficient for perceiving the existence and working of this chain, let alone breaking it. In order to cut through these links, we need to acquire Buddha's wisdom. If we contemplate upon these links according to the Right Teaching, our wisdom is sure to grow and Nescience, which we have been accumulating through aeons of ages of Blind Karmas, will gradually decrease until at last it is totally eliminated. At that moment, Enlightenment will not be far ahead.

(4) The Contemplation on Compassion

The purpose of this meditation is to eliminate Aversion or Hatred, so as to make us become compassionate, not just to our own loved ones or our own kind, but to all *Multibeings*—and without any exceptions. And so through the power of this contemplation, the Infinite Compassion will be engendered, so as to form the Infinite basis or capacity for the development of Buddha's Infinite Wisdom.

(5) The Contemplation on Buddha's Merits

To attain Buddhahood, one would need virtually innumerable Merits. Since we all have bad *Karmas* which will hinder us in attaining wisdom and realizing Buddhahood, we have to contemplate upon the Buddha's sacred Merits to help us clean away our bad *Karmas*. Also, in a more religious sense, through the blessings of the Buddhas, we can reach wisdom and Buddhahood more easily. Even if we are not able to fully understand how this blessing works, simply to contemplate upon the Merits of the Buddha is still a very pleasant joyous experience, because the Buddha Himself is a joyful figure to look at and contemplate upon.

The above is a brief account of the "Five Contemplations for Ceasing the Perturbed Mind."

—Lecture given on 10/15/1988

Chapter 6:

The Contemplation on Defilements
（不淨觀）

Right now I am going to make a more detailed account of the second item of the Five Contemplations—that is, the Contemplation on Defilements—so that we can begin to practice it today. Before we do the Contemplation upon Defilement, we need to know that there are three things most detrimental to our goal of Enlightenment. They are called *the Three Venoms* or *the Three Banes*. The Three Venoms are **Attachment**, **Aversion** and **Nescience (Ignorance)**.

You should know that if the teaching you receive, either from me or from others, is concentrated upon removing these Three Venoms, then that teaching is good and is going to lead you toward Enlightenment. Otherwise, you would have to watch out and consider the whole thing all over again. The genuine essence of the Buddha's Teaching is that if some Dharmas are devoted to the elimination of the Three Venoms, they will then lead one to Ultimate Liberation, and hence they are Orthodox Buddhadharma; otherwise, they can not be called the Right Dharma, no matter how many *tour de force* one can display—such as suspension, being buried alive, eating glass, and so on.

Among the Three Venoms, Nescience alone does not have a substantial Corpus (or Entity) of its own. It manifests itself through the other two Venoms—Attachment and Aversion. While Attachment and Aversion seem to be only two items, they can be broken down into innumerable things—such as fury, hate, irritation, hurt, harm—and even killing, which is the most violent form of Aversion. The coarsest form of the destructive state of mind is *Fury*, through whose force one explodes into tremendous anger. *Hate* is comparatively more reserved than Fury since it does not reveal itself so conspicuously and violently; it is, in a way, a strong and concealed hostile emotion. These second-generation Venoms in turn will beget all forms of other Venoms that will vitiate the mind and keep us from Enlightenment.

In Buddhism, there is nothing called "original sin" or "sin"; for in the Buddha's Teaching anything that is bad is committed due to Ignorance. For this reason, the Buddhas believe that people are educable and reformable, They *know* that **all people are *originally good*;** that their faults or evils do not come from someone else's doing, and so **there is no reason why they should be penalized for someone else's sin as their Original Sin**. It does not make sense. In fact, **their own true sins are the Venoms that they foster in their own mind**; and this has got nothing to do with others, and so nobody else should get penalized for these, either. Furthermore, their sins (or Ignorance and so on) would not disappear for someone else's death. Logically speaking, nobody can die for anyone else; and ethically, it would not sound fair and just to let someone else die for you: in fact, it would be an outrageous thing just to think and hope that way. Now let us revert to what I was saying. Consequently, as quite different from other religions' views, the Buddhas just view ordinary people as *ignorant* but *not damnable*, and They believe that *ignorant people can be educated to become wise.* So far as Mahāyāna Buddhism is concerned, everybody is teachable, even the most stupid or wicked ones, for their Nature is originally good. Therefore, *the Buddhas forsake no one* (there is no excommunication in Buddhism), *damn no one* (there is no ecclesiastical Damnation or Final Damnation or Damnation of any kind in Buddhism). In Buddhism there is only blessing and infinitely patient teaching. The Buddhas and Bodhisattvas never condemn anyone, never punish anyone. They never kill and are never killed. What they do is simply leading all Multibeings patiently towards the Road of Ultimate Enlightenment or Buddhahood for it is definitely reachable and available for all: if one sincerely and devotedly follows the teaching of the Buddha and works hard continuously, it can be done.

The purpose of the Contemplation on Defilements is to remove the Venom of Attachment from our heart. It should be noted that Attachment does not just mean being attached to something desirable, for we can also be attached to anything, either desirable or undesirable, likable or unlikable, lovable or unlovable, and so on. In fact, our mind is with such wonderful capacity and so all-encompassing that it can absorb virtually everything and anything, so that the Mind often compared to the earth. The earth can take and hold everything—whether it is clean or unclean, treasurable or abominable; the earth can accommodate them all. Although the earth can hold anything, and yet the earth itself is fundamentally unchanged and unmoved by the things it holds. Such is the same with the Mind—the Mind collects images of everything from outside and hold them there, but the Mind itself is fundamentally unmoved and unchanged in its nature just like the earth. In Mahāyāna Buddhism, the Mind is called the *Mental Terra,* and the teaching about the Mental Terra is called the Dharmic Portal of Mental Terra. If you are able to perceive your own Mind like the Mother Earth, capable of holding and enfolding everything, you are coming close to Enlightenment.

Always remember that the Buddha told us that if we wanted to practice or cultivate ourselves, we should <u>not</u> *go outwardly and seek externally*; rather that we should come back to ourselves. *Within ourselves we have everything inherently*; and so if we *really understand ourselves*, we will be able to comprehend everything. This is the key to all Buddha Dharma and *Prajñāic Wisdom*: you yourself are a self-sufficient *microcosm* (a small universe), and this very *microcosm* is the manifestation of the *macrocosm* (the large universe), which comprises all the worlds. Therefore, it is our own obligation and our own choice that we **return to ourselves in this body and this mind of ours**, both of which together are called "Me" or "I." And this "Return of the Original ME" would constitute the first crucial step in serious practice on Ch'an or Buddhism in general.

Although "I" or Ego is composed of both the Mind and the Body, the Mind is much finer and more delicate than the Body, and so without the assistance of the Eye of *Prajñāic Wisdom*, it is unlikely for ordinary people to perceive the Mind. Therefore, for beginners, let us try the "rudimentary" or more evident item first; namely, to visualize the Body at the outset. Then, what is the Body? A person without *Prajñāic Wisdom* can only view the body as "one," i.e., as *an indivisible and integrated whole*—a vague lump sum. But seen through the *Prajñāic Wisdom*, the Body can be analyzed and divided by its functions; therefore it is far from indivisible. The Body can be classified into at least six major parts: the eyes, ears, nose, tongue, body, and the Heart. The Heart or Mind here, however, does not mean the invisible Mind (or the Cognizances); it is rather the visible organ.

The six organs in our Body are also called the Six Entrances, for they enable us to reach the external world. The organs convey matter and messages between the internal and the external; thus they are indispensable in the sustenance of people's life.

When one of the Six Organs comes into contact with its corresponding Dusts in the external world, a Cognizance, or the awareness of the forms, will arise. The process of these interactions can be categorized and depicted as follows:

THE EIGHTEEN REALMS

ORGAN	+	"DUST"	→	COGNIZANCE
EYE	+	Color/Forms	→	Visual Cognizance
EAR	+	Sound	→	Audio Cognizance
NOSE	+	Smell	→	Smelling Cognizance
TONGUE	+	Flavor	→	Tasting Cognizance
BODY	+	Contact	→	Tactile Cognizance
MIND	+	Conceptions	→	Conceptual Cognizance

*The "+" sign signifies "contacting," and
 the "→" means "producing" or "Engendering."

Organ, Dust, and Cognizance are called **the Three Categories**. The Six Organs, Six Dusts and Six Consciousnesses altogether constitute **the Eighteen Realms**; whereas the first two categories (the Six Organs and the Six Dusts) are called **the Twelve Locations**.

Now, let us apply the knowledge in this chart to our meditation. In doing the Contemplation on Defilements, we generally start from the tangible items, i.e., the Six Sensory Organs, and then we will proceed to the Six Dusts, and the last stage would be the Cognizances.

Why would we contemplate upon the Defilements of the Body at all? For the strongest Attachment that can thwart us from Enlightenment would be our adamantine love for the Body. And this is also exactly why we all have a strong fear of death: because we love this body of ours so much that we could give up virtually anything for it.

If we divide the Body into the Six Sensory Organs and meditate upon the Defilements of these organs, it will help us to rid ourselves of our Attachment to the Body much more easily. However, by getting rid of the Attachments, it does not mean that we need to "get rid of the Body," but just our *Attachment to it—the problem does not lie in the Body* (the Body itself is not at fault); *the fault is in the mind!* Once we can rid ourselves of our Attachment to the body, we will be free—liberated! For example, if you own a piece of precious jewel, but you are not attached to it, you would feel free to go anywhere without being hampered by it. But to the contrary, if you are deeply attached to that precious stone, then you would not feel comfortable unless you take it with you anywhere you go, so that you can be sure that it would not be stolen or destroyed. Such is the case with this precious Body of our own: we are so deeply attached to it that we would never part with it for a second for all the world; even at the moment of death, we would still cling all the faster to it, and that is only to make the inevitable final separation more painful.

The practice of the meditation upon the Defilements of the Eye is designed to free us from our Attachment to Forms and Colors. This is the most difficult meditation, since most of what we love come to us through the eyes. And yet bear this in mind: *it is not the Eye that is at fault,* nor the Forms or Colors perceived, *but the Mind which grasps the Forms illusively!*

Therefore, ultimately speaking, instead of merely contemplating upon the Defilement or Uncleanliness of the external, we should revert our *contemplation to the internal Uncleanliness of our Mind,* because the Love in our Mind is really the root of all Attachments.

The Buddha teaches us that *there are Nine Openings in our body, and that from each of them there exudes all kinds of excre-*

tions all the time (such as *phlegm* from the throat, *sweat* from the pores of the skin, feces from the anus, etc.). None of the things excreted are pleasant to smell or touch or taste. They are, essentially, unclean stuffs. The point is that why do we love this Body that is always producing such unclean things so much? The Buddhas tells us that we love the essentially unclean Body because "Multibeings are *inverted*," (Multibeings means all living Creatures). The trouble is that we never consider ourselves inverted and that is due to our lack of awareness of the Reality of things.

To the eyes of the Buddha, all Multibeings fall a victim to Timeless Unawareness which makes them inverted in one way or another. Viewed from this standpoint, we are actually all very much alike. Therefore, in order to attain Enlightenment, we need to correct all of the Inverted Views and habits, such as Attachments, Aversion, Jealousy, and so on.

In performing the Contemplation on Defilements, as I said earlier, we would begin by contemplating upon the Sensory Organs. And then, we will proceed to contemplate on the Six Dusts, and the final items for contemplation would be the Cognizances which arise from the interaction of the Organs with their respective Dusts.

Yet today it will be sufficient for us to contemplate upon the Sensory Organs only. In fact, we might need to practice on them for quite a long while before we can be ready to proceed to the next stage—the Six Dusts. In the meantime, there is another term for this meditation; namely, the Contemplation on Bodily Uncleanliness.

Now we have learned that the Contemplation on Uncleanliness is used to bring down our Attachments. As for the power that the Three Venoms has over people, everybody varies: For instance, some people may have more Attachments than others, while still others may have in their temperament more Aversions, or Ignorance or both combined, or even all three of them, with different shades. So, the emphasis in the individual practice of meditation should be so designed as to suit different personalities. However, we would need to know as many techniques as possible so that we may select the ones that are most suitable to ourselves. Therefore, if you think that your worst weakness is Attachment, then this meditation should be the right choice for you.

In doing this meditation, start with the eyes, then proceed to the nose, then the tongue, etc. You can also meditate upon the Nine Openings (2 eyes, 2 ears, 2 nostrils, mouth, ureter, and anus). You can do it one by one, with their respective excretions as well.

There are various stages in the practice of this meditation. The most basic one deals with the Sensory Organs, which lie in the external. Then gradually, the practice may taper back to the root—from the Organs to the Cognizances and the Mind (which is the director of the Organs and the origin of Cognizances), and finally to our Original Nature, which is the fountainhead of everything. If we can get to our Original Nature, then, that would be a supreme accomplishment, indeed! We can also gradually approach the Original Nature by using the chart of the Eight Cognizances that I showed you—and such a practice is commonly done by the Bodhisattvas.

The *Ānāpānasmṛti* meditation (Mindfulness of the Breath) together with the Contemplation on the Defilement are called *the Two Sweet Dews* (or Nectars) *of Ch'an* or *the Two Dharmic Portals* of Buddhism. But you should be aware that these are fundamentally Hinayānic practices. Hinayānic practitioners wish to leave this troubled world of reincarnation so urgently, that they would like to concentrate upon the contemplation of the ugliness of the inner and outer world, so as to make themselves easier to desert it without hesitation when the time comes.

However, in Mahāyānic practice, we are not content with such accomplishments alone; instead, after the mastery of the contemplation on Defilements we would continue, in the meditation, to trace back to our Original Nature—to find out, for instance:

"Who is using the organs?

Who is using the eye to see?

Who is employing the ear to hear?

Who is moving the mouth to talk?

And fundamentally, who is using the Mind to think?—or, to contemplate?

—Who is at the back of all of these?

—Who makes all these turn defiled?

—Where does Defilement actually lie?"

We would go this far and this deep, rather than just take the "face value" of Sensory Organs, and denounce them on the superficial level. We would trace back to the root, to the very origin of them all. And this evidently would drive into the deepest core of all the issues, so that we can resolve them ultimately. Therefore it is palpable to anyone with good sense or wisdom, that this is why the Major Vehicle is, objectively speaking, much more profound and ultimate than the Minor Vehicle.

In order to benefit all Multibeings, as all Bodhisattvic practitioners do, we would need to learn all the techniques, both the basic and the profound ones. (Most importantly, please bear this in mind: 1. the Buddha does not teach the Dharma for *one person* (or *ME*) only, and 2. the Buddha Dharmas are not for yourself only! And by the way, this is also *the secret key to Buddhahood: that is, to be willing to take the trouble to learn and master all the Buddha Dharmas for the benefit of all Multibeings*—not only for myself!) The reason for this is that those who are not very sophisticated in the aptitude would need more simplified methods, since they are not able to comprehend the more advanced ones as yet. As a Bodhisattvahood practitioner, you need to be able to tell people the methods that they can really understand and benefit from them. So, as a Bodhisattvic practitioner, all the practices are indispensable, including Hinayānic ways, and we must try to master them all for Supreme Bodhi's sake.

There is a catch, though. When we have mastered the techniques, which helps us to get rid of our Attachments, however, we must not get attached to these techniques; in other words, the techniques themselves should not become our *new Attachments* after they have helped us get rid of our old ones. Otherwise it would be a very ironical situation. Nevertheless, it is tremendously difficult to transcend this irony—to practice something very arduously and become very skilled at it, and then to be able to detach oneself from the love of the things well practiced, to the extent that one almost "forgets about" them or even forget about having owned the skill. From the very start, we should be aware that these techniques are mere *tools for our Enlightenment*. ***Do not take the tool for the goal***—it is just a means. If you take the means for the goal, you will be hindered from Enlightenment by those means. The phrase "Forgetting about it" means figuratively rather than literally; it simply means *not to be attached to* the skill, but it is far from necessary to actually discard it. And so do not worry: even if you can be unattached to some Merit that you have acquired, it will still remain there, ready to serve you at any time you want—you don't have to throw it away anyhow. But that is really hard: you need to master it, use it, and forget about it, all at the same time. Yet this is just the quintessential spirit of Bodhisattvic practice—the bone marrow of Bodhisattvic Ch'an.

【 QUESTION and RESPONSE 】

QUESTION: "Can you give us an example of how the tongue is unclean?"

RESPONSE: "It can be examined from two ways in which the tongue is used. The tongue has two functions: tasting and speaking. First, in tasting, we need to chew. After being chewed, the food becomes a mess. As a matter of fact, it becomes so ugly-looking that should it drop out from the mouth, no one would like to look at it, let alone picking it up and chewing it again. Yet, what is the difference between the mess in our mouth and the mess that has fallen onto the floor? That which is in the mouth tastes really so good simply because we cannot see it. And so, we do not really know its real appearance or the actual state of its Reality: we chew and enjoy *blindly* or blindfoldedly, without the comprehension of Reality. Therefore, it turns out that we may put it this way, "To see is to disgust," or "To see the Reality is to be Detached from it." Secondly, you can also ponder over the Defilements of the tongue with regard to speech. All kinds of defiled speeches come from the tongue. These are the general ways that the tongue is to be viewed as unclean.

"And yet, similarly as I remarked above, *the problem does not reside in the tongue that tastes, nor the tongue that speaks— nor even in the food chewed and tasted, nor the speech uttered.* To drive the question home: fundamentally, **the thing that makes the tongue defiled, unclean and foul is the Mind!** And how does the Mind make things unclean? Why is the Mind unclean? It is due to *the Attachment that grows in the Mind and takes root in it,* just as weeds take roots and grow on the ground. And yet *when the Attachment is uprooted from the Mind, the Mental Terra* (the Ground of the Mind) *still remains as fair and clean as it ever is.* Besides, although weeds do grow on the soil, they never integrate and become *one* with the soil: even though the ground looks so messy because of the weeds, the weeds are never really a part of the ground—for they can always be separated. Such is the same with the Mental Weeds (the Attachments, Aversion, and Nescience, etc.) in our Mental Ground: Attachments and all the other Defilements have never become an unseparable one with our Original Mind. And once the Mental Weeds are extirpated, the Mental Ground will be restored to its Original Purity and fairness. Therefore, in the highest sense, we realize that ultimately the Mental Ground (the Original Nature) is never really defiled by the Mental Weeds (Attachments, Aversions, Ignorance, Jealousy, etc.), nor has it been actually defiled by the Three Karmas (the Physical, the Verbal, and the Mental) or the Six Sensory Organs, nor has it been virtually vitiated by the Six Dusts. The Defilements are merely superficial; they can be wiped away just as the Dusts gathered on a Mirror. Only the Wiping takes a lot of time and hard work."

—Lecture given on 10/15/1988

Chapter 7:

The Nine Visualizations
on a Corpse
（九想觀）

Besides the techniques presented in the preceding lectures, there is yet another method to meditate on Bodily Uncleanliness, to wit, the Nine Visualizations on Uncleanliness, which is also called the Contemplation on a Corpse. In this meditation, you are to visualize a corpse—which can be none other than your own body after you are dead—as it undergoes the nine stages of deterioration:

1. **Swelling Visualization**—the practitioner will visualize the corpse of a newly deceased person starting to swell, like a leather bag full of air.

2. **Blue and Mottled Visualization**—After visualizing that the corpse has swollen, the practitioner will then proceed to visu-

alize the body, being exposed to the sun and wind, beginning to change its color on the skin to leaden and blue, like someone having been beaten up.

3. **Bursting Visualization**—The practitioner, after visualizing the above, will then go on to visualize that the skin and flesh of the corpse, worn out by the elements, begins to burst and split.

4. **Blood-smearing Visualization**—The practitioner will then visualize that the corpse, with its parts and intestines scattering all over the place, is a mess of blood from crown to toe.

5. **Rotting Visualization**—The practitioner will now visualize that the body as well as its smeared parts begin to decay, and that the smell produced from the decomposition becomes more and more obnoxious.

6. **Devoured Visualization**—Now the practitioner is beginning to visualize that worms have appeared from the rotten flesh and have begun to feast on the flesh; also that vultures and animals have come to devour the decaying flesh.

7. **Dismembering Visualization**—After visualizing the flesh being consumed, the practitioner will visualize that the corpse has been torn to small pieces, scattered pell-mell all around.

8. **Bone Visualization**—And now the practitioner will visual-

ize that the scattered pieces of the corpse, with its flesh eaten up, is nothing but some piles of bones dispersed about.

9. **Burnt Visualization**—The practitioner now visualizes that there comes a wild fire out of the blue, which burns down all the bones of the corpse, creating peals of bursting noises and odious smoke. He then visualizes that finally the surrounding trees and logs and grasses also catch fire and are all burnt up together with the bones; and finally when the fire is out, there comes a gust of wind which blows the cold embers into thin air, with the sun still glowing and the water still flowing—and everything remains serene. This is the Nine Visualizations on a Corpse.

This meditation is so powerful that it can demolish our lusts and all kinds of Attachments. Needless to say, the most difficult Attachment for us to get rid of is the Attachment to the human form. As *homo sapiens*, we consider the human form as most beautiful and desirable—this does not mean just the forms of the opposite sex, but include all human forms in general. On account of this deep-rooted Attachment to this "favorite" ordinary human form, we have been detained in the Path toward Buddhahood for innumerable lifetimes. If this Love of Self-Image is altered and removed through "therapeutic" meditations, such as the Nine Visualizations, the Original Egoless Buddha Nature will manifest itself to the full, and the Supreme Bodhi will be realized.

—Lecture given on 10/15/1988

Chapter 8:

The White-Bone Visualization
（白骨觀）

Here is the detailed way to make the White-Bone Visualization: Sitting in the cross-legged Lotus Posture, the practitioner will visualize one of his big toes, say the left one, beginning to lose its skin and flesh, and finally to have only its bones left. And then he will go on to visualize that the bones are becoming whiter and whiter, as if having been bleached. The practitioner will then begin to visualize that all the other four toes of that foot have also become white bones in the same process. After that, he will visualize that all the left foot has become white bones. And then he will visualize that the calf of the left leg as well as the thigh has become white bones—which will make the whole left leg become white bones.

Subsequently, he will visualize that the right leg has become white bones in the same manner as the left one. Then the practitioner will visualize his torso becoming white bones, with the bone of the spine, ribs, and collarbones shown clearly to the eye. Immediately afterwards, he will visualize that his hands and wrists and elbows, and the two arms have turned into white bones.

Followed by that, he will then visualize that his neck has become white bones, and that his head—with the muscles, flesh and sinews and what not of the eyes, ears, nose, mouth, tongue, cheek, and hair, all disappearing—has turned into a snow-white skull. And now as a result of the foregoing meditation, the practitioner comes to visualize that all his body has become a perfect *skeleton*, and that all its bones are *bleached white*, without a stain. And he will visualize this distinctly either with his eyes closed or open. If the practitioner is able to do all these, then he has reached the accomplished state of *the first stage* of the White-Bone Visualization.

At *the second stage*, the practitioner will visualize that not only he himself has become a skeleton of pure white bones, but also the members of his family, one by one, have become white skeletons, too, exactly in the same process. And from there he will proceed to visualize that his closest neighbors have become white skeletons one after another. Subsequent to that he will visualize that all the people on the street have turned into skel-etons, and then the whole town of Carmel becomes a town of skeleton-people.

The practitioner will then visualize skeletons all over the city, coming and going, without the tendency of showing any facial expressions, but still going about all kinds of affairs—driving, running, typing, eating, etc. They look tremendously all alike, even without noticeable difference in men and women, young and old, white and black. With this accomplished, the second stage of the White-Bone Visualization is attained.

At *the third stage*, the practitioner will then visualize that the general population of New York city has become skeletons. And then New York State, the Eastern States, and finally, the en-tire United States are purely inhabited by skeletons. Afterwards, Canada, Mexico, and the whole American Continent, both North, Middle, and South Americas, together with its islands, are inhabited by skeleton people, who are hustling and bustling about, working on all kinds of jobs, transactions, and even eat-ing in the restaurants! Then Asia, Europe, Africa, and all of this magnificent Globe are replete with "*skeleton people.*" And then the *skeleton-practitioner* will visualize not only this, but other planets—and not only other planets, but also the whole Solar System, the entire Galaxy, this Buddha World, other Buddha Worlds, and all the Buddha Worlds, are all peopled by skeletons.

With these unobscurely visualized, the third stage of the White-Bone Visualization is achieved.

The White-Bone Meditation has a wonderful power to cure people of Attachments and all sorts of Illusive Differentiations. In viewing people becoming mere white skeletons, the practitioner will succeed in ridding himself of his differentiations about and Attachments to both himself and other people. Furthermore, the delusive Attachment to the human form, or to the business people do, or to the Five Desires (Property, Sex, Fame, Food, and Sleep) they seek for will all be destroyed. It would make them look tremendously ridiculous or bizarre *to do all kinds of jobs and seek for all kinds of pleasures feverishly without flesh! What good will Property, Sex, Fame, Food, and Sleep do to Skeletons?*—You might as well ask yourself and try to decipher this perplexing inquiry.

In this visualization, it is as if the practitioner were endowed with the "X-Ray Eye," which would enable him to see through the superficial layer of skin and flesh, and to see *the "Ultimate Reality" of the Bones—that all men are fundamentally alike or equal*. Hence, to the practitioner, when the Visualization is achieved, not only *the flames of his yearnings are quenched (without flesh and blood, whence comes the warmth of the body?—There would be no more fever of lusts!)*, but also the illusions of his Differentiations are subdued. No wonder the meditation of Uncleanliness (to which White-Bone Visualization belongs), together with the *Ānāpānasmṛti* (Breath-Watching Meditation) are called the Two Sweet Dews of Ch'an of the Buddha.

—Lecture given on 10/15/1988

Chapter 9:

The Five Stages in Realizing Dhyāna (Part 1)

（習禪五行之一）

In a broader sense, *Dhyāna* (Tranquility) can be used to denote either *Śamatha*, or *Vipaśyanā*, or *Samādhi*, or the total effects of them altogether. In other words, *Dhyāna* can be a general term for the various stages of accomplishments gained in meditation. For instance, the word *Dhyāna* in the title here is used in this general sense.

The Five Stages in realizing Dhyāna

There are five stages in the realization of Dhyāna:

I.   Fulfilling the Prerequisites
II. Realizing Śamatha (Cessation)
III. Realizing Vipaśyanā (Visualization)

75

IV. Realizing Samādhi (Balanced State of Śamatha & Vipaśyanā)

V. Realizing Prajñā (Transcendental Wisdom—to cleanse and transform Bad Karmas).

This list is a summary of the subjects that we are going to cover regarding meditation. It can provide you with a bird's-eye view about what takes place with meditation, how meditation should be done and how we should proceed.

However, purposefully I would like to change the order of the sequence a little bit by switching the first item to the last— that is, I would discuss the First Stage, Fulfilling the Prerequisites, at the end of this lecture for some good reasons. Therefore, I would begin with the second stage right now.

【THE SECOND STAGE】
Realizing Śamatha (Cessation)（止）

Śamatha means the cessation or halting of our restless Mind. To arrest this "monkeyish mind" we can use the various techniques already discussed before (e.g., "the Five Contemplations for Ceasing the Perturbed Mind"). Refer to my previous lectures if you wish to review how *Śamatha* can be obtained.

Our Mind is like a Lake, and the Mental Water therein is constantly disturbed; as a result, it cannot reflect images clearly;

on the contrary, it would distort the images that come to it. Therefore, our first job is to calm down the Mental Water and make it Tranquil. And then we can view things clearly and un-distortedly in the Water of our Mental Lake. The things we wish to perceive clearly are the Internal Dharmas as well as the External Dharmas.

By Internal Dharmas it means the functionings of our Mind; namely, our thoughts, judgments, and emotions, etc. Normally, in our daily life, our Mind is so disturbed and the Mental Water so muddy and blurry that it cannot reflect truthfully the images cast upon the Mind, so that we nearly do not have the slight-est idea as to *what is going on in our own Mind.* Only through the realization of *Samatha*, when the Waves and Ripples in the Mental Lake are quiet, can we have a true look at our own Mind. That means to say that only after the attainment of *Samatha* can a person really "see" his own Mind clearly. Prior to this point, all of his perceptions are either vague or distorted by the Dusts or the Cognizant Differentiations.

【THE THIRD STAGE】
Realizing Vipaśyanā (Visualization)（觀）

After attaining *Samatha*, we will be not only able to view the Internal Dharmas perspicuously, but also with the help of some special techniques, to perceive them in a *transcendental* way. In order to practice properly and effectively, we must learn those special techniques. We can learn them by studying the *Sūtras*, or by listening to lectures on them. In that way we can acquire the proper techniques as well as the applications. As a result, we would not be misled either by other people's bad opinions or by our own poor judgment.

For in the practice of Dharma, we must take the teachings of the Buddha Himself as our sole and irreplaceable guide. It is undesirable and wrong that *somebody practices on his own* or under the teachings of people who are not Buddhists, for that can be very precarious and misleading. Unfortunately, there are many seemingly good but false teachers who provide "wonder pills" that can jeopardize one's practice. Stick to the Right Dharma so that genuine *Vipaśyanā* and Wisdom can be acquired.

【THE FOURTH STAGE】
Realizing Samādhi(三摩地)

Samādhi (Equanimity) is the perfect balanced combination of both *Śamatha* and *Vipaśyanā* (Cessation and Visualization). *Samādhi* cannot be achieved if there is too much of the one or of the other. Specifically, if the practitioner has acquired too much Cessation, then his Mind tends to become too *quiet* and *dull*. At this juncture, it is necessary to *exhilarate* the mind and animate it a little bit by Visualization, such as the Visualizations of the Four Boundless States of Mind. This would prevent the Mind from being reduced to be too "submergent" and dormant like a torpid bear in the winter-time. The goal of meditation is not to become a torpid bear or a piece of log; nor is it for running away from anything. After all, semantically speaking, the word "Meditation" means "deep thinking," but not "deep sleep" or dummy-like sitting. Then what should we contemplate in our meditation after gaining tranquility through the Cessation of *Śamatha*? After the attainment of *Śamatha*, we should utilize the Tranquility gained by *Śamatha* to contemplate *deeply* on the Supreme Buddha Dharma so that it can be engraved and rooted deeply in our Ālays, the Eighth Cognizance, and finally it would form a part of ourselves. This would be the chief purpose of Visualization (*Vipaśyanā*).

If, on the other hand, the practitioner has done too much Visualization, his mind may become restless. At that time it would be necessary for him to revert to Cessation in order to quiet the Mind down.

Thus, when the mind is too dull, go back to Visualization; if it becomes too active, then switch to Cessation again. You would do this until you reach the exactly balanced point for yourself and, at that point, you would be able to attain Equanimity of *Samādhi*. In other words, there are highly sophisticated adjustments to do between *Śamatha* and *Vipaśyanā* before *Samādhi* can be reached.

Attaining Equinimity (*Samādhi*) is a proof that your meditation practice has reached an advanced level. Generally this stage is gained through continuous and perseverent sitting for many hours day and night, and in most cases, and even all through the night without rest. In other words, both Cessation and Visualization must be practiced for quite a long time and they should be fully mastered before Equinimity can be achieved. I am telling you this not to scare you or to discourage you, but to truthfully explain to you what is necessary so that you will not have any misconceptions or impractical illusions whatsoever about meditation. And the true message here is this: Meditation is not a *game* or *pastime*; it is hard and serious work for the Reformation of our own Karma, and the revolutionary Transformation of our Mind toward Buddha Bodhi. And so do not take it lightly or playfully.

【THE FIFTH STAGE】
Realizing Prajñā（般若慧）

In the wake of the attainment of Equanimity (Samādhi) for some time, *Prajñā* (Transcendental Wisdom) will arise in the practitioner's Mind. By the power of *Samādhi*, you would contemplate all the Internal and External *Dharmas*, as well as all the Worldly and Ultraworldly Dharmas at large, so that you can fully comprehend the Original Nature of everything. From that time onward, your Mind would no longer be *beclouded* or deceived, and you would be able to *transcend* the all and sundry *Dharmas*—to wit, to be able to fare free beyond the bondage of those Dharmas. That is why *Prajñā* means "Transcendental Wisdom."

Once *Prajñāic* Wisdom is obtained and put in practice to transcend the Three Venoms and all Calamities, it would then be called *Mahā-Prajñā-Pāramitā*. *Mahā* means "great"; *Prajñā* means "Transcendental Wisdom" and *Pāramitā* means "to deliver to the other shore"; altogether they mean "the great Wisdom to deliver people to *the other shore* (of *Bodhi* or *Nirvāṇa*)." "*This* shore" indicates "the Shore (or Realm) of Vexations and Afflictions." "The *other* shore" signifies "the Shore (or Sphere) without Vexations and Afflictions."

Up to now, apart from the First Stage, we have already covered four items of the Five Stages of Meditation. Therefore, let us come round to present this First Stage: "Fulfilling the Prerequisites."

【THE FIRST STAGE】
Fulfilling the Prerequisites（前方便）

At this stage of meditation, for the fulfillment of the prerequisites for the accomplishment of *Dhyāna* (Tranquility), there are three steps for the practitioner to follow. The Three Steps presented here follow mostly the magnificent teachings of Bodhisattva Nāgārjuna (meaning "Dragon Tree," *circa* 3rd. cent.) in his great work, *The Treatise on Mahā-Prajñā-Pāramitā*:

STEP 1. To denounce the Five Desires
STEP 2. To renounce the Five Shrouds
STEP 3. To execute the Five Cultivations

Dhyāna is, as mentioned before, the broadest term used to indicate the various accomplishments gained through meditation. If someone has attained *Dhyāna*, then he is regarded as an accomplished practitioner in meditation.

These things are called Prerequisites because they are the Requirements for practitioners to fulfill before they can authentically set out to realize Dhyāna. Hence, these are indispensable for the serious meditator, especially for those who are aiming their goal at Enlightenment and true Wisdom.

It is understood that there are some people who are interested in meditation merely to improve or enhance their physical health—and without a doubt, meditation, if done properly, is capable of doing that. Whereas some others would practice meditation in order to escape from the daily affairs for a while to relieve the stress of a busy day and, as it were, to recharge for the next day. But these "Utilitarian Meditations" are not the types of meditations we are talking about. Here we are majorly concerned with, so to speak, the *traditional orthodox* meditation which has been handed down to us for more than two thousand years. And so this is the serious genuine meditation for true Buddhist practitioners, and not for amateurish dilettantes. Even though we might have numerous Karmic Obstacles, yet that is no excuse for not doing our very best to conform to the Authentic Teaching as we possibly can, so as to make our efforts worthwhile.

【 STEP 1 】

To denounce the Five Desires (訶五欲)

The first Prerequisite in the first step for realizing *Dhyāna* is to denounce the Five Desires. Some Masters in the past used to inculcate that we must avoid or even forsake Desires, but it is very difficult for us to do it that way now, since our world is getting more and more complicated, and our Desires are getting more and more multiplied, and as a result of mass production and swift communication, people's Karmas are getting much heavier than ever. Therefore, I would say that instead of total renunciation, merely "to denounce the Five Desires" would be the more feasible practice for people today. To worldly people, Desires are usually considered as enjoyable and good. But as genuine meditation practitioners, we should not look upon Desires as proper objects of pursuit. If we practice meditation while secretly clinging to the Five Desires and pursuing them as fervidly as usual, then the effect of that meditation would be marred or totally ruined, so that it might not be beneficial to us at all.

There are two genres of Five Desires. The first genre consists of the Desire for:

1. Form
2. Sound
3. Smell
4. Flavor
5. Touch

These items sound somewhat abstract and metaphysical; nevertheless, they can also be quite concrete and tangible once their meanings are explicated and well understood. They are explained as follows:

(1) The Desire for Forms（色欲）

Although usually the term "Form" can include all kinds of Forms, or tangible and visible things, for meditators, the Form denotes especially Human Forms of the opposite sex (i.e., the male or female body). This desire for Human Forms, apparently, is one of the strongest for sexual desire which is based on the Desire for Forms, and it turns out to be the primal cause of Reincarnation. Furthermore, sexual Desire is one of the most formidable factors in disrupting a mind for Tranquility (*Dhyāna*).

(2) The Desire for Sound （聲欲）

As Ch'an practitioners, we should not become attached to any type of sounds, especially pleasant ones. There is a story concerning five hundred advanced meditators who, through the advanced achievement of meditation, had acquired the ability to fly in the sky. While flying over a Royal forest, they happened to hear the songs of the king's concubines who were bathing in a pond in the forest. Upon hearing the sweet voices of the concubines, the minds of those meditators were greatly moved and disrupted. At that very moment, the practitioners lost the power of control of their *Dhyāna*, which soon vanished into thin air. In the next moment, they all fell down to the ground!

Thus, pleasurable sounds can be very hazardous distractions to practitioners of *Dhyāna*, and so as such, it should be denounced.

(3) The Desire for Smell（香欲）

The desire for good odor can be a strong distraction to *Dhyāna* practitioners, too. Another story goes like this: Once there was a pond with some lotus flowers and water lilies blooming beautifully upon it. A *Dhyāna* master chanced to come that way and ran across the pond. At the sight of the magnificent lotus flowers, he was greatly enchanted. He could not help standing there watching and sniffing, nearly totally forgetting about what he had been up to. At that instant, the Floral Goddess reproached him in exclamation, "Don't you steal my Fragrance!" On these words, the Dhyāna master "awoke" to himself; but he protested, "Why would you say that? I was not stealing anything since I did not take anything from you." The Floral Goddess replied, "Yes, you did—you were grasping the colors and forms with your eyes and the fragrance with your nose. By watching and sniffing so avariciously, you were at the point of losing your Dhyānaic state of mind, if I did not come to warn you in time."

(4) The Desire for Flavor（味欲）

Flavor has something to do with the tongue and the enjoyment of food and drink. When you are meditating, do not think about food at all. During meditation, if you happen to smell the food that your wife or your neighbor is preparing, do not be ensnared by the smell or get distracted to begin to pounder over what is going to be served for the supper and how savory it is going to be.

(5) The Desire for Touch（觸欲）

Among the Five Sensations, Touch or the Tactile is the one that has the strongest connection with sex. Although there are several kinds of Touch, the most difficult form to overcome is the Tactile associated with sex. As meditation practitioners, we should be very consciously aware of the power of Touch in disrupting meditation.

There is a legend concerning an advanced meditator who lived in a remote mountain. One day the king of the country, hearing about the accomplishments of this practitioner, sent his messengers to invite him to the palace as an honored guest. The king wished to pay homage to the practitioner and make offerings to him. To the king's great pleasant surprise, the practitioner flew to the palace, and the king was overjoyed and received him with great honor and made generous offerings to him. Since then, the practitioner came at invitation to the Palace in this way several times. One day, the king asked the queen to pay homage to this practitioner. In doing so, the queen prostrated before the practitioner and touched his bare feet, as was the custom, to show her highest respect. The queen's hands felt very soft over the meditator's feet, and the practitioner, not having had that kind of experience before, suddenly felt very excited at the touch, and all at once he lost his *Dhyāna*. Subsequently, he felt dizzy and exhausted and his body became very weak. As a result, he was no longer able to fly and had to request a carriage from the king to transport him back to his mountain retreat! So, this is the hazard of Touch to a meditation practitioner!

The above have been the First Set of Five Desires. Now let us turn from the Metaphysical genre of desires to the more tangible, materialistic ones, that is, the Second genre of the Five Desires; namely, the Desires for:

1. Wealth
2. Sex
3. Fame
4. Food
5. Sleep

The reason why I reserved the First Stage to the last is partly because this Stage demands a much more thorough discussion, and partly because it touches upon some sensitive parts of our daily concern; i.e., about money, sex, food, fame, etc. *At the mere mentioning of these items, Meditation has become not just some exotic, far-away, mysterious Oriental curiosity, but something highly close in contact with our day-to-day life.* In other words, to discuss about these Prerequisites, you would come to realize that Meditation is not merely a wild fantasy, which you can partake at will like seeing a movie in whatever way you like.

Rather, *by discussing these Prerequisites, meditation will become very realistic and highly serious.* If you want to get the genuine stuff, the Real McCoy, then ***you need to live up to it***. Although, for sure, you may not be able to do it a hundred percent well, at least you would know what is *good and genuine practice* and you would also know exactly what you are doing. Furthermore, with these Right Views as the guideline, you could march toward the Right Path without any doubt.

(1) The Desire for Wealth （財欲）

Wealth indicates money and property. During meditation one should not think of or dwell on wealth or property. But this is not enough; in fact one should not practice meditation for the purpose of gaining or accumulating money or property. If one does, one would fall into the snare of Māra and go astray from the Dharma.

(2) The Desire for Sex （色欲）

This is particularly one of the reasons why I delayed this discussion until now. Although people everywhere love sex, it is beyond a doubt that Western people *now* tend to *overstress* its importance in *worldly happiness*. And "sexy" has recently become a professed *eulogy for a* "*virtue*," which is still unacceptable to most Eastern people. This is a modern mundane thinking. But Ch'an practitioners, it seems to me, need to contemplate this from another angle, and to perceive it more deeply, too. If we can avoid sexual activities, then we could become more spiritual. Apparently, this is a very difficult thing for the laity to do, and they do not need to do it if they do not want to. However, to be very frank with you, *the avoidance of sex is crucial to proper meditation.* Meditation is like charging our "battery," and if the battery is fully charged, the light that it powers will illuminate brightly. However, if we drain our battery through sexual activities, we would have defeated our purpose of meditation.

If you wish to reduce or eliminate sex, it is essential that you *get the agreement and understanding of your spouse*; *do not cause matrimonial problems because of your meditation practice*! That is not true Buddhism; *Buddhism means to seek peace and to solve problems*—both inner and outer, and *never to cause problems.* If your spouse does not approve of a reduction or elimination of your sexual activities, then that is partly due to your own *Karma*! You are not entitled to blame it on the other party. On the other hand, if your spouse approves, then that is owing to your good *Karma* in past lives! Concerning this point, all that you can do is simply take advantage of whatever you have right now and do your best to improve yourself, so that you can have a better inner life and family life as well. This is one of the most predominant features in Mahāyāna Buddhist practice:

never force anything to happen egotistically; always take other people into consideration in whatever you practice.

Of all of the desires, Sex is by far the strongest and the most difficult one for meditation practitioners to cope with, since Sex encompasses all of the first set of Five Desires that we have discussed (Form, Sound, Smell, Flavor, and Touch). And in the course of Sex all of these Desires are present simultaneously in their most poignant forms. Besides, we need to be always aware that it is the Attachment to Sex that we are continuously subject to interminable Retributional Reincarnations.

If you are unable to totally renounce Sex as yet, you might be able to reduce the frequency of your sexual activities to be less than that of the regular people who are not meditators. At any rate, you are expected not to lead a voluptuous life while practicing meditation: to be a Buddhist meditator, you should at least evince more spirituality than ordinary people do.

(3) The Desire for Fame（名欲）

As I have mentioned before, the underlying reason for many of the pursuits that people undertake in this life is ultimately directed toward Fame. Fame includes praise, honor, respect, adoration, worship, and even power and control. When an ordinary person fails to get respect from others, he would feel as if all that he owns and everything that he has accomplished become useless or meaningless. Thus, people's goal in obtaining *the material* is ultimately for the sake of *the immaterial*. And among the immaterial questings, Fame, along with Riches, serves as the most powerful drive for life.

In the Ch'ing Dynasty (*circa* 1700 A.D.) in China there was an Emperor called Chien Long. Once during his pleasure trip to the south, while he was observing the many boats sailing back and forth on the Yangtze River, he remarked to his Prime Minister about how gorgeous the numerous boats were. However, the Prime Minister replied that there were only *two boats* upon the river. The Emperor, somewhat angered by being contradicted, demanded his Prime Minister to explain how did he mean that there were only "two" boats upon the river. The Prime Minister said, "Your Majesty, there are only *the boat of Riches* and *the boat of Fame*." During most of ordinary people's lifetime, just like the boats upon the river, they constantly travel back and forth in a hurry seeking mostly these two things—Wealth and Fame, together with all the *variations* and *by-products* of these two, such as power, worship, woman, territory, supremacy, enduring everlasting name, and so on, and so forth. Indeed, these are the most heart-throbbing unquenching lusts and quests and dreams to most Mundane people.

(4) The Desire for Food（食欲）

A person who wishes to practice meditation seriously cannot be a gourmand or glutton. He cannot be finicky about food and cuisine. He should not give himself up to gluttony, either. He is supposed to eat the proper amount and at the proper time. In one word, he should eat moderately. However, to go fasting all day long is not the Buddhist way, either, because it would revert to the other extreme of gluttony. The authentic Buddhist Way is always the tranquil, balanced "Middle Way," which calls for a perfectly balanced peaceful mind, in good keeping with Dhyāna (Tranquility), and which is totally against any kind of Extremity or Fanaticism. But you should know that it is much easier to do thing in the fashion of ups-and-downs Extremity, and that the Perseverance and Tranquility in sticking to the Middle Way is really hard: The ordinary people (including some other religions' adherents) tend to go to the extreme (for instance, the Fasting of the Hinduists, Taoists, Muslims, and the Lent fastings and Carnivals of the Catholics); only the Saints are capable of taking the Middle Way.

(5) The Desire for Sleep（睡欲）

In order to practice meditation seriously, a practitioner is required to sleep as little as possible. The Buddhist meditator can eat as much as is needed for his physical health, but if possible, he should try to stay awake all the time. This is Buddhist practice and it is different from many other religions' practice. Some other religions' instructions are just the opposite, such as the Taoist's or some Hindu's teachings. They say that it is all right to oversleep yourself, but you should try hard to refrain from food altogether, and eventually you are expected to go total fasting for a long period of time, such as several months or a whole year or more. And it is deemed as a Virtuous deed or great practice. In Buddhism, however, we do not advocate total fasting due to the fact that people do need energy to practice meditation. In fact, Meditation is a very energy-consuming activity. Besides, fasting in itself would never improve or enhance Wisdom in any way and could not do any good whatsoever to Enlightenment. At its best, total long-term fasting is a deed of self-negation and self-mortification, if not self-torture, but it is never a deed of Virtue or Wisdom, maybe just the opposite of it.

As your practice improves, you will find that you need less and less sleep and your time for sleep is naturally reduced before you are aware of it. Now let us contemplate upon Sleep by asking: "Who is sleeping?" You may answer that it is your body that is sleeping. However, in reality, the body does not *need* any sleep at all. It is *the Mind* that needs it. The mind needs sleep to rest because of the Karmic result of Nescience (Ignorance). Nescience is like a big benighted black hole that can engulf everything in darkness. In the course of our daily life, we would accumulate all kinds of Karmas that would afterwards be deposited entirely in the Mind. And these deposited Karmas would form a heavy shroud over the Mind, so that we would feel dark and heavy and sleepy at the end of the day. And so we would retire to sleep. Then in the sleep, these Karmas would be pressed down to deposit in the lower realm of our Mind—the Ālaya (which is like our "subconscious" or "unconscious" Mind). After the Karmas have settled in the Ālaya, the surface of our Mind would then become clear and lucid once again, and so we would wake up "in a fresh mind," as if we had been revived. Once awake, we would begin anew to commit and accumulate some more Karmas which would once again settle into the Ālaya Cognizance during the next sleep—and so, in this way, our ordinary life goes on and on. This is the function and position of Sleep in an ordinary person's life.

There is a term in Buddhism called "Turbid Submergence." When we are upset, we feel *low* and *sunken* (submerged) in spirit and our mind becomes *dull* and inactive. Besides, when we feel bored or ennuied, the Mind would also become dull and dormant. These phenomena are called Turbid Submergence. Sleep is the strongest kind of Turbid Submergence. During meditation or in a lecture in the class, if one feels a little sleepy, it is Turbid Submergence in the lighter form; when Turbid Submergence becomes strong and heavy, it would make one go to sleep. To sum up, Turbid Submergence is the result of daytime accumulation of

Karmas on the surface of our mind that shrouds our mind up to make it become dark and dull and low.

Therefore, if we wish to practice meditation seriously, we need to overcome the Shroud of Sleep to stay consciously aware at all times.

The above has been the denouncement of the Five Desires, as the Step One of the First Prerequisite for the Fulfillment of *Dhyāna*. We will continue to discuss the other two steps in the next lecture.

—Lecture given on 5/20/1989

Chapter 10:

The Five Stages in Realizing Dhyāna (Part 2)

（習禪五行之二）

Now, as a review, let me reiterate the first Three Steps of the Prerequisites for the Fulfillment of *Dhyāna* in diagram consecutively:

STEP 1: To denounce the Five Desires（訶五欲）

There are two genres of Five Desires:

(A) The Metaphysical genre:

The Desires for

      1. Form

      2. Sound

      3. Smell

      4. Flavor

      5. Touch

(B) The Materialistic genre:

The Desires for
>   1. Wealth
>   2. Sex
>   3. Fame
>   4. Food
>   5. Sleep

As these two genres of Five Desires could prevent us from concentration and would veil the clarity of our Mind, we should denounce and restrain these desires.

STEP 2: To renounce the Five Shrouds（棄五蓋）

The Five Shrouds are:
>   1. the Shroud of Avarice
>   2. the Shroud of Aversion
>   3. the Shroud of Sleep
>   4. the Shroud of Exuberant Levitation
>   5. the Shroud of Skepticism

STEP 3: To execute the Five Cultivations（行五行）

The Five Cultivations are:
>   1. the Cultivation of Aspiration
>   2. the Cultivation of Remindfulness
>   3. the Cultivation of Diligence
>   4. the Cultivation of Ingeniousness
>   5. the Cultivation of Unitary Mindedness

【 STEP 1 】

To denounce the Five Desires (訶五欲)

This is the section that we covered last week. We talked about "denouncing the Five Desires" and explained how those "Five Desires" could destroy or obstruct our ability to concentrate ourselves properly in meditation. Just one more word. By "denouncing" or "chastising" it connotes the practitioner's ability to view in perspective that the Five Desires are undesirable and a hindrance to the purpose of his practice, so that he either chastises himself for having such impure desires, or treats the desires, if any, as "personified beings" and reproaches them so as to hold them down or banish them; that is, to get them out of the way. So much for Step 1. Now I am going to discuss Step 2 "To renounce the Five Shrouds" as the second prerequisite for the Fulfillment of Dhyāna.

【 STEP 2 】

To renounce the Five Shrouds (棄五蓋)

There are five kinds of "Shrouds" that can envelop our Mind in the pitch of Ignorance; they are:

(1) The Shroud of Avarice
(2) The Shroud of Aversion

(3) The Shroud of Sleep
(4) The Shroud of Exuberant Levitation
(5) The Shroud of Skepticism

By "Shrouds" it means that these dharmas can muffle up our Mind's Eye as well as our Original Nature. The reason why we have drifted away from our Original Nature is mostly due to these "Five Shrouds." Nevertheless, we are actually never far from our Buddha Nature—it is always there with us; still we could not see it, owing to the "Shrouds" which envelop it from our sight. We are on one side of a "wall" and our Buddha Nature is on the other. The wall of the "Shrouds" stands between us and our Buddha Nature. It is this untransparent "wall" that makes us feel that we are far away from our Buddha Nature and from all the Merits and Wisdom. But as a matter of fact, we are very close to it indeed! It is important to remember that we are not at a distance from our Buddha Nature at all, and that the obstacles separating us from it are not as great as we think them to be. Our goal is to remove the "Shrouds" so that our Buddha Nature can be revealed. The techniques are discussed as follows:

(1) To renounce the Shroud of Avarice（棄貪蓋）

This is, in one sense, a summary of the first step in "The Prerequisites for the Fulfillment of Dhyāna"—to denounce the Five Desires. Only this time, the practice would go deeper, and the practitioner would deal with the Five Desires with a final blow, so to speak. The Five Desires, or the Shroud of Avarice as called here, are so deep-rooted in us, for we have been accumulating these *Karmas* for such a long time that they have become almost impregnable and extremely hard to remove or get rid of. Therefore, right after finishing the First Steps of the Requirement, it is beneficial for us to make a further endeavor, almost like a final combat, or the terminal scuffle in bayonets on the front line, so as to insure that all the remaining enemy (baneful roots) are done with in all their trenches and battlements. In other words, to renounce this Shroud of Avarice is to "finish them up," to do away with the Five Desires once for all.

(2) To renounce the Shroud of Aversion（棄瞋蓋）

When we have a liking for something, we tend to grow attached to it. If, however, we cannot obtain that which we desire, then that feeling of Attachment rebounds to become a feeling of Aversion or Detestation. These feelings are very pernicious to meditators—even much more so than Attachments are. For Attachments can drive us to do good, bad, or neutral things, yet Aversion or Detestation can only goad us to do injurious acts—it is purely negative and harmful in its nature and function. As a matter of fact, most of the destructive deeds in the world are done directly or indirectly through the urge of anger, Aversion, or hate. Hence, it is imperative for the practitioner to remove the Shroud of Aversion.

Incidentally, among the Three Venoms, Nescience (Ignorance) is the primitive origin of all the pernicious things, and Avarice or Attachment is its "first generation offspring," while Aversion or Hate is the "second generation." Together, they form a "family"—the home or originators of *Samsara* or Reincarnation.

(3) To renounce the Shroud of Sleep（棄睡蓋）

Sleep is considered as a Shroud because it can veil up our Consciousness in utter darkness. In the sleep, we usually totally lose control of ourselves and the power of volition. People in the sleep are, according to the *Sūtras*, very similar to the existence right after death (specifically, the 49 days interim between death and rebirth, i.e., *Antara-Bhava* in Sanskrit), for after death, we would lose most of our mental power, especially the power of volition and, at the same time, our *Karma* will take over and make all the decisions for us, and we will be thus willy-nilly led to our next Rebirth.

In the sleep, due to different previous Karmas, some people would have nightmares, others would have pleasant dreams, while some very good practitioners would be able to continue practicing the Dharma to some extent, even in their dreams! It sounds fantastic and incredible, but it is not. The fact is that these people who have been practicing the Dharma very hard, upon encountering some difficult situations or calamities in their dreams, they may either invoke the Buddha or resort to the Dharma by reciting a *Dhārani* (*Mantra*) or some paragraph from text of the *Sūtras*, or do something helpful (as compared with the total helplessness of ordinary people), and their predicaments calamities in that particular dream will vanish or be resolved presently.

Nevertheless, this waking life of ours is something like a dream, isn't it? Therefore, the dream we have in the night is, so to speak, *a dream within a dream*, which is just as in *Hamlet*, where we have "plays within the play." Similarly, we have "little dreams" within the "Big Dream." However, most of us here, I presume, would like very much to awake from this "Big Dream" and that is exactly why we are here studying Buddhism. (For to be awake from the dream means to be *enlightened*.) However, most of us are drawn here to this class by our mutual *Karmic* force; and most of the time in our life we are driven by our *Karmic* force, knowingly or unknowingly.

As practitioners, we would feel unhappy about the fact that sleep often reduces us to sheer powerlessness and helplessness, like a living corpse. It is for that very reason that the Buddha admonishes us not to sleep too much. Furthermore, the Buddha taught us that, as Buddhist practitioners, while we should eat sufficiently to maintain our energy for practice, we should yet try to sleep as little as possible. Sleep darkens everything; it is professedly one of the worst three enemies for meditators, the other two being the Aberrational Agitation of the mind and Exuberant Levitation. When you are doing very well in your practice, and then suddenly, for some reason, you stop to sleep, afterwards when you wake up again you would find, to your lamentation, you must begin anew with your meditation practices—for the continuous progressive line has been broken up or interrupted by the "blank" or disturbance of the Sleep. It is somewhat like driving a car on the highway: if you make a stop in order to take a rest or do some other things, and afterwards, to get on with your journey again you need to restart and rewarm up the vehicle and re-accelerate all over again.

Notwithstanding, *you should not force yourself not to sleep.* If you do, then you may find that the next day you might justify yourself to sleep even longer for compensation's sake—for you might unconsciously feel as if you had been maltreated or abused by yourself!

If you wish to test the quality of your practice, a very good way to do so is to assess it by the amount of sleep that you need. If your practice is progressing well, you would find that you gradually need less and less sleep. This sounds rather mysterious but it is not. You can understand this fact by the working of the Shrouds. If you fully comprehend the nature and functioning of the "Five Shrouds," you would be able to perceive the mystery of sleep. The mind needs sleep because, after a whole day's gathering for the "Five Dusts," it is covered with thick layers of Dusts and is, therefore, tired and heavy. We need Sleep in order to clarify the mind by allowing the dusts to settle into the *Ālaya*; that is to say, to put them away in the storage, like our daily inventory. Proper meditation practice could clarify the Mind without the necessity of taking much sleep. Meditation here acts like a good agent or an organized storekeeper who usually keeps all his stock in order, so that he actually needs very little time to stock the new inventory. Besides, the entire stock is always in good order, neat, and effective. Thus, with the help of meditation our mind would not be messed up with untidy Dusts; therefore, it is obvious that it no longer needs the same amount of sleep in order to organize and clarify itself. Consequently, you would feel wide awake and your Mind could always stay very conscious and clear.

There are times, however, when you would feel the need for more, rather than less, sleep after practice. But honestly it is not due to your laziness or tiredness. The reason for this is that, during practice, you are cleansing your Mind of Impure *Karmas*. Cleansing the Mind of Bad Karmas is somewhat like sweeping the floor of dust. As you sweep the floor in order to make it clean, the sweeping may raise up some Dusts which will soar onto the air. Thus, sometimes after a cleaning of our Mind of

Bad Karmas, the "Dust" we have swept into the air would seem to becloud our Mind even more, and we would feel unusually sleepy as a result. At that point, we should not give in to sleepiness. We should try hard to get up and walk about a bit in order to dispel the feeling of Sleepiness.

(4) To renounce the Shroud of Exuberant Levitation
（棄掉舉蓋）

Exuberant Levitation is excitement or high in spirit which would make one restless. We need to eliminate any Levitation or Restlessness that exists in the Mind. In meditation, we would try to avoid any excitement or "high" in emotion which could result in Restlessness, so that we would be able to calm our mind. Levitations generally come from two sources: the recollections of *the past* and the expectations for *the future*. Both of these can throw you into the abyss of regret, remorse, nostalgic lamentation, worry, anxiety, and even never-ending reveries. In one word, this is the ailment of failing to stick to the conscious track of *the present*. Therefore, in meditation be sure to stick to *the present,* and never dwell on the future or the past, for we need to come to the realization that the past was "deceased," and the future is yet unborn—the deceased past is but a shadow or unsubstantial specter and the unborn future is a figment of our imagination, and none of them has any real Entity right now—so it is pointless to dwell on them and to be beguiled by them which are no more than Illusions or Delusive Images conjured up by our own Mind. To contemplate in this way, our mind would be able to stay tranquil and free from Levitations (undue excitements) of any kind.

(5) To renounce the Shroud of Skepticism（棄疑蓋）

There are four kinds of Skepticisms or Doubts: the Doubts about the Buddha, the Dharma, the Saṃgha, and oneself. The first three of these together become the Doubts about the Three Precious Ones.

a) The Doubts about the Three Precious Ones

If you have any Doubt about the Three Precious Ones (the Buddha, the Dharma, and the Saṃgha), especially about the Dharma, it would cause tremendous Hindrances to your practice. In some gravest cases, it might even totally disable you in practice. Among the Doubts about the Dharma, the most serious one is the Doubt about the *Tathāgata Nature*, or the *Buddha Nature*, or *Original Nature*, because if this Doubt arose, then all the Buddha Dharma in you would be annihilated to the last shred. For without the Buddha Nature, nobody could ever become a Buddha, and it follows that all the efforts of hard practice would be meaningless and futile. And this is called by the Buddha the most Evil View, for it keeps everybody from the quest of the Supreme Bodhi and to remain forever Ignorant and at the mercy of everlasting *Samsara*.

Therefore, we have to eliminate Doubts concerning the Dharma, or the Teachings of the Buddha, to the extent that we deeply believe that *the Dharmas are good and are able to lead us to Nirvāṇa and the Supreme Enlightenment.*

b) The Doubts about Oneself

This means the Doubt about one's ability to practice, or specifically, to attain the highest goal—and in this case, it means to attain the Supreme Bodhi, *Anatana-Samyaksaṃbodhi*. If we have any doubt of this sort, then it would certainly hold us back in practice, and we would not exert ourselves to do our level best for it—because we could see no hope for us: You seem to say to yourself: "No, I'm not made for this; not ME. This is much too high a goal for me." or "That's too perfect for me." This would mean the lack of self-confidence. And it would amount to nothing but heaps of *excuses for laziness and evasion.* But this Self-doubt is against the first doctrine of *Buddha Dharma* that ultimately all Multibeings share the same quality of Buddha Nature, and that *eventually you will also become a Buddha yourself (otherwise the Buddhas and Bodhisattvas should not bother to come to inculcate us so patiently time and again).*

In the last analysis, all the Self-doubts arise from the *Karma* of Nescience (Ignorance), the Ignorance about the Ultimate Truth. And this Ignorance has been repeated and accumulated for such a long time that it has become a *Karmic Habit* to us, so that we have become ever ready to revert to it "spontaneously," should we consciously try to illuminate or change the habit in any way. But this Karmic Habit of Nescience is so much against the Ultimate Truth, and so much in the way of our own Enlightenment, that we need to change it by all means, if we are to hope for any significant fruition in practice in this life-time at all. Otherwise, all the practice would be very flimsy, for, after all, even as common sense goes, Self-Confidence is the basis for any kind of enterprise. Therefore, the elimination of any Doubt about yourself—*your ability and your potentials*—become the most crucial point of your practice. You should so educate yourself and reform your own pattern of thinking in this line that you could be spiritually and mentally *correspondent to* the Higher Dharma.

This has been the Second Step of the Prerequisites for the Fulfillment of *Dhyāna*: to renounce the Five Shrouds.

【 STEP 3 】

To execute the Five Cultivations (行五行)

The first two steps of the "Prerequisites for fulfilling Dhyāna" are truly "prerequisites" as such; in other words, they are outfits you need to be equipped with *prior to* your actual commencement with "serious meditation." Thus the Third Step stipulates the things you need to do both *before* and *in* meditations:

(1) The Cultivation of the Aspiration for Dhyāna (欲)

This means primarily the Aspiration, or Wish for attaining the *Dhyānic* state. We need to deliberately instill this Wish into ourselves, for if we do not have the Wish for *Dhyāna*, we would not be able to attain it. We must enhance the Desire for the *Dhyānic* state as strong as possible, so that we would strive as hard as we could in order to attain that state. The stronger the Aspiration is, the higher the attainment we can achieve. If our Wish is weak, then our attainment will be limited, because Wish is the origin of Will. If we have a very strong Desire to attain *Dhyāna*, then we stand a very good chance to attain it sooner.

This Wish, however, is never *inherent*. This is one of the most important parts of Buddhist Teaching: *Anything good, or any "Good Root," is learned, practiced, cultivated and acquired;*

nothing is inborn and obtained effortless, and nothing is condoned to you by any Super Being. You should work for it. In Buddhist Teaching and Wisdom, *no one is born a Saint or Bodhisattva or even Buddha.* **Buddhahood or Bodhisattvahood comes exclusively from Wish, Will, practice, perseverance, and the conquest of difficulties.** Nothing comes from nothing. *The higher the goal, the more effort it requires.* Partly because of the fact that the attainment of *Dhyāna* is hard, and partly due to our previous Impure Karmas, *we tend to grow lazy and become smug with the little we have achieved*, and so time and again we need to *prompt ourselves* to cultivate higher and stronger Wishes for the *Dhyāna*.

Therefore, if you have a Wish or Aspiration for *Dhyāna*, you must try to make that Aspiration stronger and stronger—no matter how strong it already is, there is always room to enhance it! We all need to strive very hard to do this.

(2) The Cultivation of Remindfulness（念）

Once we have made the Aspiration for *Dhyāna* as strong as we could, we must then keep that Aspiration always in our mind; we must not forget it for an instant—this is important, but believe me, it is no easy task to do! Because of our Karmic Habits, we tend to forget *good* things very easily! And yet we have a strong tendency to remember *bad* things and cling to them tenaciously. It just so happens that no sooner have we learned some good things than we would forget about them.

Here let me use an analogy of a man wandering in the desert to illustrate this point. When this man comes upon a pond of water, he rejoices and bends down to drink of the water. Before he can drink at all, however, he must first brush aside the leaves and debris that are floating upon the surface of the water. After his first drink, if he wishes to drink again, he must brush the undesirable stuffs aside once more—for they have resumed to the former state to cover the surface of the water. The leaves and debris are likened to our Karmic Dusts, and the Pond to our Original Nature. Our Pond of Original Nature itself is always clean, but it is "undrinkable" (that is, not readily for use), until we brush aside the Karmic Dusts or debris from the surface. Once we have done this, then we could take a drink from our Pond of Original Nature (i.e., it can have its full and free play of all its latent potentials—not a bit of its energy is wasted, trammelled, or covered up—and this is called LIBERATION). But like leaves and debris, the Karmic Dusts would cover up our Original Nature again and again. And they must be removed again and again so that we may continue to drink from the Pond of Original Nature, or to make it "useful." To keep the Mental Water drinkable, we must constantly brush aside the Karmic Dusts. If we stop brushing the Karmic Dusts away, we would quickly miss the delicious "water" of our Original Nature. Therefore, if we stop our practice (brushing aside the Karmic Dusts) for just one moment, then our Mental Pond (Original Nature) would soon become untidy again. Consequently, it takes continuous efforts to accomplish the goal of *Bodhi*, and Remindfulness has a significant role to play herein.

(3) The Cultivation of Diligence（進）

Diligence is one of the most important factors in Buddhist practice. Just as a student who works hard will earn his degree more quickly than one who is slack in his studies, so too, if we work hard, we will attain *Dhyāna* more quickly than if we are lax in our practice.

Sakyamuni Buddha relates the story about Himself that in His past lives, a long time ago, when He was still an ordinary lay person, Maitreya had already avowed and started his Bodhisattvahood practice forty *kalpas* (eons) before Sakyamuni did. And yet, says the Buddha, Maitreya "took it easy" and did not strive hard for his aim. Later on, Sakyamuni finally made up His mind for the Supreme Bodhi, and He strove so hard and worked so diligently that He attained His Buddhahood even before Maitreya, who was supposed to become a Buddha first. This means that by His Diligence, Sakyamuni has surpassed more than forty *kalpas'* time and thus shortened the length of time to His Buddhahood, as well as abbreviated ages of unwanted Afflictions and Rebirths, both for Himself and for innumerable other Multibeings. Therefore, Diligence is an imperative factor that can expedite the achievement of the ultimate goal.

(4) The Cultivation of Ingeniousness（巧慧）

This means that you must objectively compare the Merits of the *Realm of Dhyāna* with the demerits of the *Realm of Desire* ours in order to promote your Wish for *Dhyāna*. Visualization will help at this point. You could visualize how joyful you would become after you attain *Dhyāna*; also visualize how joyful the Buddhas and Bodhisattvas are in their State of *Dhyāna*. Therefore, the cultivation of Ingeniousness is to exhaust all the skillful means to strengthen your will to attain your goal. Where the will is fortified, the True Way is bound to reveal itself.

(5) The Cultivation of Unitary Mindedness（一心）

By Unitary Mindedness it means to fix your mind fast upon your meditation. Do not let your thinking *disperse* or wander; when it does, you need to **pull it back** again even by force. However, before you can pull your mind back to the right track, first of all, you should be able to be *aware* of the fact *that your mind has wandered away*. Most of the times we are unaware that our mind *has* gone astray. Once we are consciously *aware* of its having wandered apart, we must force it back again. And this is going to happen ever so often that we would find ourselves repeat the same effort.

It is important that you are *not to be discouraged* about this, for it is merely Karmic Habit that causes your mind to wander astray. With time and practice, you will improve and your mind will wander less and less, until it is finally fixed at one single point, which is the realization of the initial *Dhyāna*.

【CONCLUSION】

These have been the three groups of "Prerequisites for Dhyāna," and they are really the key or "secret" to *Dhyāna*, too. To sum it up once again, they are the prerequisites for serious meditation practice, and indeed, for "Professional Meditation" also: Without conforming to these we would be merely "Amateurish Meditators." There is no *short-cut* to *Dhyāna*; if any, this is it.

Yet, this is not an easy path, for there is no Path is ever easy. But fortunately, at least now we know the real right way to Dhyāna. This is the original, the genuine, the authentic Buddhist Teaching concerning meditation fulfillment. Meanwhile in the practice of meditation one should look out for the Three Deceptions:

1. Not to be deceived by others.
2. Not to deceive ourselves.
3. Not to deceive others.

All of these are difficult to avoid. If we do not wish to be deceived, then we must have the first-hand knowledge about the true state of things; that is, not to practice merely by hearsay, but by the genuine teachings of proficient, experienced teachers, and preferably from the *Saṃgha* masters (Buddhist priests). We must have the proper "know-how" so that we would not be misled. This is true not only of Westerners, but also of Orientals. In

Taiwan, China, America, and elsewhere, there are a variety of practices preached by many "teachers" with "supernatural" powers. It is easy for ordinary people to be deceived by charlatans. Innocent people are especially more easily to fall a victim to them due to gullibility derived from lack of genuine knowledge about the Dharma.

Secondly, we must not deceive ourselves. Many practitioners tend to deceive themselves into *overrating* their own accomplishments. Again, this is the outcome of being ignorant about the true state of things. Once we succeed in deceiving ourselves about our own achievements, then it would become fairly easy for us to deceive others. That is why on this globe right now we have so many "Living Buddhas" or "Saints" who have founded so many different sects with numerous followers. To be free from self-deception is to be delivered from the Timeless Ignorance, which will result in penetrating and evaporating all the falsehood of phenomena as well as the illusion of the *Expansion of Oneself* and its encroachment upon others. Once the self-deception is ultimately extirpated, we would be able to witness our "Original Visage" for the very first time. And this is much to be anticipated.

Thirdly, in order not to deceive others we must be able to detach ourselves from self-deception, as well as from the attachment to wealth, fame, prestige, respect, and the like. *Any form of Buddhist practice that concerns itself with the acquisition of money or fame is bound to be false and destructive.* The Buddha himself has told us that to practice Buddhism for this purpose is to follow *Māra's Karma* (Māra meaning evil-doer or demon) and to become *Māra's* Cohort, both figuratively and literally. In sum, to be able to transcend the Three Deceptions, one needs to acquire great Wisdom, so as to see through all sorts of trickeries, delusions and illusions, both internally and externally.

[*The Meditation Session Begins.*]

[*After the Meditation Session*]

You may have noticed that, immediately after a deep meditation session, you would not wish to talk. This is due to the quietude of your mind that takes place as a result of meditation. This quietude in the mind is so strong that you do not feel like opening your mouth or bestirring your Mind for speaking. Partly for that reason, after sitting meditation, we would need to practice some walking meditation, so that we could "recover" to our normal physical and mental state.

—Lecture given on 5/27/1989

Chapter 11:

An Epilogue:
The Legend of Running Meditation and the Incense Board
（跑香與香板之源）

About 260 years ago, in the early Ching Dynasty in China, there lived an emperor called Yong Cheng who was very domineering politically and rather devoted to Buddhism. Once, the emperor sent for a Ch'an priest named Tien Huei (meaning "Celestial Wisdom"), who had received the Transmission of the Chou-Dung Sect of the Ch'an Denomination, to discuss the Dharma with him. Upon speaking about the High Dharma with this high priest, the emperor at once realized that the monk did not seem to know the Essentials of the Dharma at all and had not yet experienced Enlightenment. Because Yong Cheng took the Dharma very seriously, he became exceedingly angry with the monk and said, "We will give you seven days to relate to me what the Essentials of the Dharma are. No one can decipher the Essentials of the Dharma unless he is enlightened. And we are going to send a guard to keep you under surveillance, and if you cannot tell us the Essentials of the Dharma by seven days, the guard will chop your head off!"

In olden times, if a monk was enlightened, he would not be afraid of anything and even emperors would prostrate themselves before him and honor him as Master of the State. But, of course, this monk in question was not yet enlightened, so he could not but go into strict retreat in order to get the right answer and save his own head. Later on, the emperor became a little lenient and told the monk that he would allow him twenty-one days instead of a week to find out the Essentials of the Dharma.

In the first seven days of his retreat, Tien Huei did not sleep at all—he could not! Instead, he vigorously meditated to pursue Enlightenment, for his life was at stake! He practiced extremely hard for he knew that the emperor meant what he said.

In the next seven days, again he did not dare to sleep, but practiced even more strenuously. By the fourteenth day, due to lack of sleep, he began to feel drowsy and sleepy and sometimes he would fall asleep for awhile. But if that happened, in no time he would start up as from a nightmare, and he would begin to walk around the room in order to drive the sleepiness away.

During all this time, the guards took turns to stand sentry at the door to his hut day and night—these might be the guards who would behead him at the emperor's command if he failed in his quest for enlightenment.

On the fifteenth day, Tien Huei walked on in order to drive away the sleepiness so that he could continue with his meditation. On the sixteenth day, Tien Huei became extremely anxious so that he began to walk more quickly. On the seventeenth day, he walked even faster—gradually the walk developed into a slow running. By the twentieth day the monk still had not attained any Enlightenment yet.

On the twenty-first day, still anxiously striving for Enlightenment, Tien Huei ran faster and faster, and the more anxious he grew, the faster he would run, until suddenly, somehow, he bumped into a wall. His head was bruised and cut and bleeding a little, and he fell down onto the floor. At that very moment, all of a sudden, he said, "Oh, I see!" Tien Huei then tranquilly told the guard that he wished to speak to the emperor. The emperor, hearing this, realized that Tien Huei had achieved Enlightenment which made him a real Master.

This tale connotes two messages: first of all, when a person's life is at stake, he would undoubtedly practice very hard. Secondly, it also shows that although Enlightenment could come most unexpectedly, and yet it would not occur without tremendously painstaking efforts. After the enlightenment, Tien Huei eventually became a Patriarch, and the practice of Running Meditation (called *Pao-Hsiang* or "Running Incense" in Chinese) became a tradition in the Ch'an Hall. This legend is also the origin of the "Incense Board." The Incense Board is in the shape of a sword, which figuratively threatens to chop one's head off if one does not try hard to practice for the achievement of Enlightenment! Besides, the sword also symbolizes the Sword of Diamond-like Wisdom which could serve to cut through the tenacious "cobwebs" of Timeless Ignorance and Illusions.

—Lecture given on 5/27/1989

【 APPENDIX 】

An Echo

(1) A Letter from a Reader (an inmate in a California prison) of Jan. 20, 1997

Dear Rev. Cheng Kuan,

I hope this letter finds you well and happy. I read the book from "The Dharma Banners Series" called "The Sweet Dews of Ch'an", Lectures on Buddhist Meditation given at Chuang Yen Monastery, N.Y.

In section #3. on page 26 and part of 27 I learned that the minor vehicle has limited compassion, they are egoistic, They will not attain ultimate enlightenment. Lets see, they

123

are Dormant, seemingly expired, I see the word self-obsessed. "That's nice".

The Buddha had this thing in his teaching called the Noble Eightfold Path, and in this, their [*sic*] is a thing called <u>Right Speech</u>. I am sorry to see the Prejudice feelings you hold.

Did you know that the Buddha was an Arhat? I would be happy to tell you where you can read it in the Tripitaka.

Why do the Mahayana schools teach people that the Hinayana and other Buddhist schools are no good?

If the Theravada were Communists like the Mahayanas to the North of them would you accept them as your Brothers then? Are people from Ch'an Mahayana or Great Vehicle?

Why does their [*sic*] have to be labels on what is good (Buddhism) like the label Great Vehicle or minor vehicle? Why do you have to be better than them? Can't <u>them</u> be welcome by <u>WE</u>? If we say White is better than Black we would have Prejudice, and here in America people look <u>down</u> on it.

With all of your wasted words that are full of hate and Prejudice towards your fellow man [*sic*], and through not knowing what you are doing because of Ignorance you are giving Buddhism a bad name.

All of the major traditions (sects) should try to join hands in Brotherhood.

The Dhammapada says in [#]134 "If, like a broken gong, you silence yourself, you have approached Nirvana, for vindictiveness is no more in you.

I understand many of my words go deep but they are man to man and not mass-produced in Literature to show whole world how big a Fool I really am.

Thank you, with metta

B. Y.

(2) A Response from the Author of Feb. 1, 1997

Dear Mr. Y:

Thank you very much for your letter of Jan. 20, 1997. It seems to me that it is very good and laudable for a person in your situation to be interested and so serious about Buddhism. In this letter I would just like to clarify some points:

Let me ask you some questions, if I may. First of all, "Is an Arhat the same as Buddha?" If yes, why were the 1250 Arhats, who usually accompanied the Buddha, not called Buddhas? Next: "Why even the Ten Great Disciples, the greatest Arhats of all Arhats, kept on learning from the Buddha throughout their lives, long after they have obtained their Arhathood?" And thirdly, "Why is it that even recorded in the Sūtras that the Great Arhats kept coming back to the Buddha for instructions concerning something they were asked?" Therefore, an Arhat is not the same as a Buddha: *Arhathood is not the same as Buddhahood.* An Arhat has much much more to learn before he attains Buddhahood, if he wants to. Therefore, *the Buddha was an Arhat, but the Arhats were no Buddhas.* And let me ask you another question: "While the Buddha was called an Arhat, does it mean that He is *just an Arhat*?" The fact that He was *ALSO* called an Arhat was simply because it denotes His capacity for Nirvāṇa. Now, another question: "Do you know, besides Arhat, the Buddha is also called *Tathāgata, Samyaksaṃbuddha, Vidyā-caraṇ a-sampana* (knowledge-conduct perfect), *Sugata* (well-departed), *Lokavid* (knower of the world), *Anatara* (the peerless noble one), *Puruṣa-damya-sārathi* (the tamer), *Śāstā Devamanusyānām* (teacher of devas and men), and *Bhagavān* (World's most venerable)? These, together with *Arhat*, are the Ten Holy Epithets of the Buddha, which He has earned through His attainment of *Samyaksaṃbodhi* (the Ultimate Enlightenment).

With respect to the terms Mahāyāna, Hinayāna or Greater and Minor Vehicles, I wish from all my heart that there have not been such differences in Buddhism. However, one thing very good about Buddhism is that although we may have different opinions about practice, but we can discuss, or even argue, but *we never Kill*. Throughout the 2000 years of Buddhist history, Buddhists do not kill each other on account of different opinions, neither have they forced anyone to accept their belief, or try to covert others by force or by worldly lures. By the way, these terms, which make you so mad, were *not my inventions*; they were *the Buddha's words in the Sūtra*, if you read much enough, you would know.

Now, why is Mahāyāna superior to Hinayāna? As I said, I wish they were the same, they were equal. But they are not. You know why? It is because of *Intention*. As I said above, if an Arhat wanted to, he could practice more and attain Buddhahood. But usually he would not, and that is why he remains an Arhat.

For he would rather be an Arhat and get into *Nirvāṇa* at the end of this life. You know why? Because he has not begotten his *Bodhicitta* (the "heart" or Intention, or determination to attain the Supreme Bodhi). And why not? Because the attainment of the Supreme Enlightenment takes *numerous lives* of endeavor to practice both for one's own good and simultaneously to benefit Multibeings by teaching them the Way of Enlightenment. And this involves **Great Compassion** for the sufferings of Multibeings. But an Arhat would not do so. He would rather get into *Nirvāṇa* right away, and never to come back again, even though this world is full of ignorant people, like me, who is craving for instructions from great masters. But my ignorance and my suffering are my business; an Arhat would not care less, so long as he himself can stay safe and sound, calm and cool in his *Nirvāṇa*.

However, the practitioners of Mahāyāna, who are called Bodhisattvas, the Saints of Mahāyāna, act very differently from the Arhats. In order to emancipate people from their Ignorance, Avarice and the pains of Transmigration, they all make solemn vows to come back to this world. They don't forsake people to enjoy their own tranquility once they have acquired the Way of *Nirvāṇa* or Emancipation; on the contrary, they would feel that they are needed all the more, and they can offer more for people's Dharmakaya or blessing. And so, they take the trouble to help people learn to attain Enlightenment, and they would do this not for just one life, but lives after lives and ages after ages, *just for compassion's sake*, and just because he would never forget that he himself had been in the same needy and helpless situation before. Therefore, since Buddha and all the Saints have helped to liberate him, he, now turning a Bodhisattva himself in turn, will help others to get liberation. And so, it turns out that it is not simply because of Compassion that he is willing to help, but also because of **gratitude: it is a way of expressing his gratitude toward the Buddha**, so he will follow the exact steps of the Buddha, to instruct and liberate people, whatever it takes. By so doing for innumerable lives, this Bodhisattva, will have accumulated innumerable Pure Merits which will entitle him to Buddhahood. **If the Buddha was like most other Arhats, there would not have been such a thing as Buddhism which we are fortunate enough to learn and practice.** We are fortunate due to the Great Compassion of the Buddha and the Bodhisattvas, so that we would not be deserted as helpless orphans (just like the Arhats have deserted us). For this reason, "the Lesser Vehicle" is far from a "label" that is imposed upon them; rather it is a categorical nomination derived from the Buddha to denote a state of mind with less compassion, and less care about people's sufferings. This is why the Minor Vehicle is inferior by its own attribute—this has nothing to do with prejudice; it only has something to do with facts and limitation of the mind and compassion and the will to choose. Mr. Y, please don't take it for granted that there is only one kind of Buddhism; in fact, there are many, if you read more, you would know.

Talking about prejudice. Are you a prejudiced person, Mr. Y? Are you prejudiced against Whites (or Blacks)? Are you prejudiced against Orientals? If you were not, then what has made you ask for a free gift (i.e. the free book you have requested and received from me), and having received a free gift, slap right in my face with my free gift, and twisted and smashed the contents of my free gift—that is, what has embolden you to write me such a rude letter? If you don't know I am an Oriental, would you be so rude enough to do it? It is rude and unfair.

Finally, I am very sorry to say that, with all my ignorance (which includes sending you books free), I have not made you happy and satisfied, but have made a fool of myself in front of you and all the world. My sincere apology.

Sincerely yours,

Cheng Kuan
Abbot of A.B.T.

P.S. ① No matter how many names you have called me, but in the Mahāyāna belief that all men have Buddha Nature (which is the basic teaching of Mahāyāna), and so, eventually you will be enlightened to become a Buddha yourself, wouldn't it be a nice thing? Besides, do you believe that all men have Buddha-Nature? If you do, that's great, and maybe we can talk more.

② At any rate, I think Buddhist practice is great, and it will help you out or tide you over in your adversity, especially in your present situation. I do sincerely wish that you will do well in the prison, so that you may get out of it quicker and have a new and better life (If you come out, I would like to see you very much). In your situation, the practice of Buddhism, like I said, is very good and precious, be it Mahāyāna or Hinayāna. But let me give you a suggestion, don't just as yet get into argument about sectarian differences and be militant in spirit, keep practicing and read more, don't jump to conclusion; lay aside your prejudice, and read more; later on you will be able to make a wise decision . If you choose Theravada, that's fine. But just don't slander me or anybody.

③ Don't take other people's kindness for granted. Especially strangers'. Nobody owes you anything. And you tend to see hatred in things where there is no hatred, and see prejudice where there is none. It is nothing but a *revelation of your own mind*: when a person's mind is full of hate and prejudice, it is *reflected* in everything he sees. And sometimes the hate and prejudice is so full in the mind that it overflows in whatever he sees and thinks and says. And you have a strong inclination to think, not with your head or reason, but with your feelings or sentiment. That's why you are being muffled in your views by your sentiment, and you are not able to see things properly and clearly, only vaguely and distortedly. On that account you are so very easily beguiled and misled by your own sentiment, yet still feel yourself justified, and always feel wronged by all the world. That explains why you are so head-strong and rash, so immature and childish about things. More importantly and fatally, you carry this mental habit into the practice or reading in Buddhism: viz., you don't practice with your head or reason, but practice with raw sentiment, that's why you find it difficult to calm yourself down.

④ Finally, Mr. Y, please don't quarrel with me or with anybody about sectarian doctrines, because you really know far too little to do that. For instance, do you know although the Mahāyāna and Hinayāna people do argue with each other throughout ages, but they don't quarrel like *foes* or enemies, and the other party is never *damned* in words or actions. And the arguments even never get into a fist-fight, let alone fighting with weapons (It is unimaginable to see two Buddhist monks beating or kill-ing each other to "defend" their own doctrines—*in the name of the Buddha*!) Indeed, they argue just as civilized scholars would do, or at the worst, they simply squabble *like brothers* in the family. In fact, their contention is very much like a *domestic squabble.* And so any outsider who does not understand tries to mediate or meddle or fool with it, is a fool. Because just like family, we love and respect each other, for we are truly blood and kins, although we don't totally agree with each other, as brothers usually do. And so, like brothers, we never in a moment *wish the other to perish, or try to exterminate each other.* Quite to the contrary, with all our differences, *we always wish the other to flourish and prosper*! And so until now we still have standing international organizations for all the Buddhists in the world, and the delegates from all over the world meet annually to communicate and discuss matters for the well-being and propagation of over-all Buddhism. And this is something quite "incredible" to other religions, wouldn't it? Consequently, to fully comprehend Buddhism and to practice it well and properly, it is not just in the reading of a couple of small booklets, or pamphlets, it takes enormous endeavor to study and comprehend numerous original texts of Sūtras, and to immerse oneself in the whole background of culture of that area, so that one can get a clear and correct picture, without any misunderstanding or misinterpretation, or self-supposing distortions.

(3) The Reader's Response

Dear Rev. Cheng Kuan,   2-8-97

Thank you very much for your letter and....

Thank you for opening my eyes and removing the thick layer of dust that has been covering them.

I now see that I should slow down and think about what I read, and yes you are right, I really don't know enough to argue with anyone of your expertise.

I am sorry for rude and unkind letter that I wrote you and hope you can forgive me.

The book I talked about in the letter is in fact an Outstanding and helpful meditation Darma [*sic*] teaching and I am very sorry I misread part of it.

You have <u>NOT</u> made me unhappy or unsatisfied.

And NO you did not make a fool of yourself in front of me and the world. <u>In fact</u> I am the real fool in my own little world.

You asked me if I believe that all men have Buddha-Nature. Well, <u>if</u> I remember right the Buddha discovered that every man has the same basic ability not only humans but all sentient beings possess the same Buddha-Nature. "Sure I believe that all men have that quality!" Some (<u>like me</u>) will take a little longer, because of the many years of evils or "aKusala Karma". I know I will have to go through at least another life before I become Enlightened because the life I took in this one, and all that I stole and the countless animals & insects I killed.

I have been in prison & jail for over 8 years and have converted to Buddhism a year and a half or so ago.

I sure wish I would have found Buddhism many years ago, because if I did, I sure wouldn't have caused so much suffering....

When it comes to meditation I have what is called a Monkey-mind, I'm sure you know what that is. In fact, unless it is very quiet I have a hard time reading, it's like I start reading and as I go find myself daydreaming as my eyes are moving on the words in the book that I am reading, then I have to back way up to where I started from and start over - then over until I sit [*sic*] my book down and try again later. (I never give up however).

Maybe it has a lot to do with my location. Here in prison I listen to every sound I hear and always watch eyes of other convicts wherever I walk. It is hard to find quiet, there is quiet but I am usually sleeping then because I have to go work early in the A.m., and quiet is from 12:00 ^{Am} till 6:00 ^{Am} or so.

Well, I will try to work out a time schedule for meditation. And speaking of time, I better cut this short because I'm sure your schedule is very busy.

Please accept my apology for the very negative words that were in my last letter.

If there is ever anything I can do for you from inside these walls, please just ask.

Truly yours,

B. Y.

P.S.   I will now start with Anapanasati.
P.S.#2 An Arhat is <u>Not</u> a Buddha. ☺

About the Author:
The Venerable Cheng Kuan

1. Currently:

Abbot of Americana Buddhist Temple (Michigan) and Mahavairocana Temple (Taiwan), 1991–

2. Experience in Buddhism:

- Became ordained Buddhist Monk in 1988, under Master Hsien-Ming (45th-Generation Patriarchate Holder of Tien-Tai Sect)

- The 53rd-Generation Acharya of Shingon Sect, Koyashan, Japan (1996–)

- The 42nd-Generation Lineage Successor of both Hua-Yen and Sole-cognizance Sects (2010–)

- Commentator of *The Suraingama Sutra*, et al.

- Translator of *The Lotus Sutra*, et al.

- 3-year Buddhist Retreat in Dallas, Texas (1984-1987)

3. Birth and Education:

- Born 1947 in Taipei, Taiwan

- Graduated from English Dept. of Taiwan Normal University

- Passed the Entrance Exams of 5 Graduate School in Taiwan, and studied in Taiwan Univ. (1977–1978)

- University Fellowship at Graduate School of English Dept., Texas Christian University (1979–1982)

4. Occupations & c.:

- High-school English Teacher (1976-1978)

- Columnist and Special Correspondent at Dallas for The Chinese Business News in Houston (1980-1982)

- Membership of Chinese Youth Writers Association (1966-1968)

- 2nd place at English Poetry Writing Contest at TCU (the awarded work, "The Tempestuous Night," a 300-line poem, 1980)

- Supervisor of English Dept. Assoc., Leader of Reading Club, Soccer team player, 2nd place of English Poetry Reciting Contest (1968-1972)

- Chairman of Creative Writing Club, School Soccer team player, Chorus member, Harmonica Team member, Leader of English Conversation Club [in high school]

5. Publications of Writing and Translation:

■ Chinese:

A Commentary on The Lankavatara Sutra; A Commentary

on Suraingama Sutra (2 vols); *A Series of Commentaries on Heart Sutra; The Treatise on the Portal of Mahayanic Centidharmic Apprehension; Logicism in Buddhism—A Commentary on The Tractate on the Right Truth through the Comprehension of Causality Logicism; A Commentary on The Thirty-Gatha Tractate on Sole-Cognizancism; A Commentary on the Tractate upon the Contemplation on the Factors Adhered to; A Commentary on The Gatha for the Operating Patterns of the Eight Cognizances; A Series of Commentaries on Terra-Treasure Pusa's Dharmic Portal; The Metamorphic Vestiges in America: a Collection of Speeches on Buddhism* (2 vols); *The Sweet Dews of Ch'an;* and *My Progress In Learning Esoteric Buddhism,* 17 items in all.

■ English:

The Sutra of 42 Chapters, The Diamond Sutra, The Heart Sutra, The Altar Sutra, The Sutra of Consummate Enlightenment, The Sutra of Terra-Treasure, The Lotus Sutra of Wondrous Dharma, The Sweet Dews of Ch'an, Three Contemplations toward Buddha Nature, and *Tapping the Inconceivable,* 10 items in all.

釋成觀法師簡歷

1. 現 任：

◆台灣大毘盧寺及美國遍照寺住持

2. 佛學經歷：

◆1988年於紐約莊嚴寺依天台宗第四十五代傳人^上顯^下明老和尚座下披剃出家

◆漢傳東密（印、中、日）三國傳燈・高野山眞言宗第五十三世阿闍梨(1996-)

◆華嚴宗兼唯識宗第四十二世法脈傳人(2010-)

◆楞嚴座主

◆法華譯主

◆美國德州閉關三年(1984-87)

3. 生平與學歷：

◆1947年出生於台灣省台北市

◆1972年畢業於台灣師範大學英語系

◆1977考取五所研究所（台大、師大、輔仁、淡江、文化），後入台大外文研究所攻讀

◆1979申請到美國三大學之獎學金，後入德州TCU英研所爲全額獎學金研究員(Fellowship)

◆1980參加校際英詩創作比賽第二名(得獎作品名「暴風雨夜」，係三百多行長詩)

◆1982於TCU修完學分，寫完論文，提出未果，尋閉關而放棄

4.經 歷：

◆（台北石牌）美國海軍醫院器材保養組夜班班長（1969-72）

◆國防部光華電台新聞官、編譯小組小組長(1974-76)

◆屏東大同國中、台北光仁中學、中山女高英文教師（1976-78）

◆休士頓「華商報」專欄作家兼駐達拉斯特派員（1980-82）

◆中國青年寫作協會會員(1966-68)

◆師大「英語系學會」監事(Supervisor)、「讀書會」主持人、英語系足球隊隊員；英文小說創作比賽第二名、英詩朗誦比賽第二名(1968-72)

◆師大附中「文園社」社長、附中足球校隊、附中合唱團員、附中口琴班團員、附中英語會話班班長

5.著作與翻譯：

◆中文著述：

楞伽經義貫、楞嚴經義貫(上、下)、心經系列、百法明門論今註、因明入正理論義貫、唯識三十論頌義貫、觀所緣緣論義貫、八識規矩頌義貫、六離合釋法式義貫、北美開示錄(一、二)、地藏法門系列、禪之甘露、我的學密歷程等中文著作共十七種

◆英文譯著：

The Sutra of 42 Chapters（四十二章經英譯），*The Diamond Sutra*（金剛經英譯），*The Heart Sutra*（心經英譯），*The Altar Sutra*（六祖壇經英譯），*The Consummate Enlightenment Sutra*（圓覺經英譯），*The Sutra of Terra-Treasure*（地藏經英譯），*The Lotus Sutra of Wondrous Dharma*（妙法蓮華經英譯），*The Sweet Dews of Ch'an*（禪之甘露），*Three Contemplations toward Buddha Nature*（佛性三參），*Tapping the Inconceivable*（入不思議處）等英文譯著共十種

Donors for Publishing the Seven Books:
大日經疏、大乘百法明門論今註、觀所緣緣論義貫、
華嚴法門集要、禪之甘露、佛性三參、入不思議處
助印功德名錄（以上七書各敬印二千冊）

台幣部分：（NT$）

50000元：許雯雯、劉秉融　43000元：陳淑慧　40000元：謝程雯　24300元：張晏城　20000元：胡煇夏　10000元：故黃炳誠、李岳鴻、胡娸靜、張育賢、許順良、郭春梅、蘇晏慶、蘇楊金蘭、蘇榮瀧、郭東義　7500元：華梵大學佛學系大二班、康李春美　6000元：洪楊設、胡麗春　5600元：張怡雯　5000元：王定國、李淑媛、柳阿呆、黃文隆、黃忠川、趙文瑋、劉婺宜、劉銘哲、潘美鳳、賴淑卿、謝秀萍、倪劉花柳、謝玉卿、林麗貞、涂陳小禮、歐宗輝、徐大智　4500元：沈蒼元　4150元：鄭宇村　3500元：施秉宏、馮翰琦　3000元：釋印雲、王明華、陳右勳、蕭吳幼、鍾福見、張進財　2800元：劉昆明　2500元：林昭銘　2500元：釋真際、釋真諦、釋普慧、釋真行、故明返、故林雨記、故康秋雄、王慧娟、何秉修、杜建權、李宪平、林沛君、林秀靜、林針、林清城、林清碧、邱瑋、高嘉鴻、張正一、張麗雲、陳裕仁、游竣安、馮振堂、葉芳琴、趙爽妙、劉筱平、陳美紅、蔡林靜玉、蔡淑卿、蔡滿、鄭金幸、賴貴英、簡木源、王興車、陳春生、林麗梅、董嘉祥　2300元：三寶弟子　2000元：王聰海、沈陳阿碧、沈登法、林春繡、姜素霞、張延夫、葉俠均、龔紹淵、故陳天三、釋玄定、惠元中醫、萬俊榮、故曾萬金、故陳卓怡君　1800元：程誌廷　1500元：朱勝美、康銀甌、陳榮燦　1250元：故廖清申、廖李貞　1220元：信眾合供　1200元：張燦同、廖啓信　1100元：陳德翰、陳德駿　1000元：故方秀英、故詹李葉、王伸權、王金瑛、王靖心、王靖彤、王豔玲、江玉雲、江秋虹、何政夫、吳桂英、李書萍、沈世權、沈靖倫、沈靖唐、沈靖皓、、林月娥、林素美、林雅雯、孫大倫、張家才、張淑如、曹秋藝、許芳嘉、許建新、許耀華、陳光懿、陳志明、陳周秀英、陳纏、黃子竣、黃育萍、圓慧、葉津杏、劉美李、蔡政良、蔡鎮州、藍國明、顏瑤玲、鐘月珍、李金興、鐘依真、游民陽　900元：劉千維　800元：孫啓茗、李平祺　700元：何欣穎、何薜濱　600元：杜旻華、林素燕　500元：釋如證、釋見卉、法藏書齋、何宗武、吳佳勳、李美雪、李榮興、林立靖、林莉娜、林莉麗、林劉健、故陳忠志、秦珮瑩、秦維均、秦雲錚、張孝慶、康經營、陳世珍、陳志賢、郭冠廷、陳張連對、劉金濃、劉惠美、歐如花、蔡佳志、蔡朝賜、賴明桂、周美枝、黃昱仁　400元：廖春來、劉玉英　300元：李丞軒、李宗易、李秋蓉、林來受、張英豪、張耀享、陳怡靜、劉啓聿、劉啓瑋、謝東山、李維仁　250元：吳建明、故王金傳、故王游春子　200元：呂家慧、林士堯、邱金滿、施怡如、康雨洶、康芷嫻、康詠舜、康經世、康經國、陳怡君、郭峻霆、郭庭好、陳富雄、陳詠瑋、郭銘哲、廖品修、蔡孟軒、蔡芳庭、鄭蕙馨、羅罵僎、羅郁棠、林佩潔、曾崇寗、曾陳乾湖、曾麒軒　100元：呂王錦秀、呂有財、呂百勝、呂沅廷、呂家華、康雨健、康柏彥、陳彥任、郭淑梅　50元：龔鈺傑　30元：蔣張文里

人民幣部份：（CN¥）

100000元：居正林　50000元：張宇　25450元：陳澤鋒　10000元：王懷祿、朱晶晶　7000元：楊成　5000元：陸美、張競文、肖西豹、郭金基　4000元：孫靜　3500元：故石占德　3000元：孫振舉、轟嚴君、孫銘浩、陳桂榮　2900元：梁瑞　2600元：王桂芝

143

（瀋陽）　2500元：鐘尚霖、胡楊　2000元：釋圓理、張靜雲、朱立春、楊光榮、楊光群、故胡月兒　1500元：戚澤林、章賦　1460元：肖惠銖　1435元：正法船流通法寶收入　1400元：謝晴、李淑華　1300元：張濤、故王湄、故王瑞芝、隱名氏　1250元：劉穎梟　1200元：孟亞莉、古京英　1150元：隱名氏　1100元：劉芹、王若西　1085元：張桂玲　1050元：萬雪康　1000元：許朝垠、隱名氏、林建兵、裘彬、張一新、張娜、徐艷娟、張狻猊、林英、故肖桂成、夏青、胡曦寧、　隱名氏、賀玉芬、錢乃光、王麗琴、錢暉、劉春、向永碧、故張早生、故陳錦秀、故張盎龍、故楊銀金、故李仰曾、故梁家蘭、故李金屏、張冬平、李梅、張煒奇、江秀英、馮勝、韓玉玲、吳玉涌、胡紅杰、王靜（青島）、蔣曉峰、李娟、毛恩華、方夕剛、徐國峰、任繼宏　　975元：張淑德　920元：何龍昌　900元：覃曉菲、覃亞文、李霞、冼玉琪、劉先平　890元：師義　850元：周瑞蘭　800元：故張屯生、王昱涵、李牧民　750元：孟保臣　710元：李文浩　700元：秦文韜　695元：黃小珂　625元：釋真體　600元：夏藝庭、隱名氏、陶宇紅、張興艷、呂捷、張蓓蓓、呂曉茵、呂曉梵、呂夢楠、王秀雲、李濟生、王胤旭　570元：董廷方　510元：故王學榮　500元：釋智開、李鑫宇、崔中旗、鄔繼艷、吳桂彩、鄔洪剛、曹勇、戚同光、陳碧如、駱錦玲、陳婭、故黃秀蘭、趙錫期、趙強、黃思超、張東旭、劉玲、林鰍、張誠、任燕、張海燕、王清芬、秦爽、秦士興、劉榮煥、康燚、魏玉鳳、魏玉珍、趙来榮、李蘇、黃海陽、洪霄、付彬、張琛、李亞紅、張淑琴、楊運、許小芹、楊倫、江秀如、江秀雲、張沃明、耿依心、楊明、張國華、故張志強、程雷、余國華、余方村、薛學琴、故原淑舉、馬永萱、于文君、宋惠林、宋瑜、孟玲茹、李直、聶若文、何孝英、郭風琴、秦梅、羅曉琳、王凌波、李鳳滿、繆盛、余世江、故袁梅魁、蔣蒔梅、張丹青、故侯樂林、張奇志、張淑蘭、呂卓凡、　陳少濱、能揚、丁思源、李莉英、李明旨、王宏敏、孫貴福、王淑芬、陳泓羽、孫慶軍、孫慶輝、徐淑英、張鳳玲、柴立俐、戚萬寶、張益銘、蘇丹梅、孟靜　490元：何明靜　454元：羅騰飛　400元：葉子非凡、故黃秀珍、故王琴珍、吳敏、崔淑權、李佳（上海）　360元：王秀江　300元：釋聖悟、釋通德、釋傳開、釋大政、梁捷理、趙世實、張靜、故趙亞鳳、朱菊英、劉靜、李淑紅、馬華偉、許歡麗、馬天嘯、黃秋玲、隋瑞娟、蔡喜娜、馬玉雲、朱春惠、朱弘義、董寶銀、向正瓊、張杰、　張春艷、李雲昌、陸美娟、付麗芝、毛玉明、故陸尚智、故黃儉、故黃洪生、故張雅芳、故顧能靜　290元：馬一鈞　275元：劉紫旗　255元：陳國昌　254元：魏敬濤　250元：朱治科、朱毅、張淑珍、孫小淼、張高昇、楊淑華　210元：黃軍敏、代永會　200元：故蔡延祝、陳穎、侯華玲、張錦程、隱名氏、陳草、陳春燕、黃錫樞、陳自強、故董大爲、張輝、張智博、陳赴蒙、陳逸、陳林、趙梓名、朱琴芬、張國琴、李群、陳曉雲、蘇祥輝、吳青原、王慶、林玉蘭、陳嘉、故吳寶蓮、張炳炎、張澤坤、吳越紅、張顥覺、徐璐、蔡義恒、張艷杰、蔡喜良、胡曉輝、胡育堂、蔡玫娜、蔡偉翔、故韓淑清、孫宗燁、馬增奇、韓桓、李稻、李楨、羅培榕、李英偉、杜詩鴻、余浩嘉、張海帆、隱名氏、王俐瓔、郝時運、楊晶晶、王晶、梁寶禮、張曉榮、李春英、李春鳳、回麗讓、朱春洲、陳依明、陳秋、吳淑釵、董輝、吳淑瓊、董是磊、李淑藍、鄭杰、唐溥成、滕剛、滕驊瑩、許智剛、祝海波、付軍、趙俊杰、尹洪琛、孫靜波、姜方文、故劉菊珍、王鋼鍵、于麗君、于芳旭、王旭、故李成實、故李王氏、故李一平、故張美英、故陸金根、故楊瑞青、故汪洪才、范度苟、范祖芳、故劉淑霞、周婉芳、黃喜英、故陸擁軍、王立一、邊柯瑋、江涵、李佳（江蘇）　175元：故尉殿雲　170元：寧志芹　160元：楊樹維、袁玉遮　150元：釋通離、楊平平、隱名氏、李振紅、曹初松、胡元英、史月娥、劉利、曾鳳英、王鐸　140元：唐海峰、陳昱宏　132.7元：隱名氏　125元：吳梅金　110元：宋玉環　101元：葉定珍　100元：高玉、魏惠瑤、魏鄭寧、謝國鈞、瞿恒、李華、田偉、陳健、陳一銘、仇笑梅、夏林、彭雅琴、劉志超、靳青梅、王紅霞（天津）、戚恒博、戚穎、張媛媛、李新宇、屈保華、陳柏宇、陳劍、馬振熙、馬寧雲、虞和定、虞和武、虞華芳、虞賽月、姜禮志、李遠靜、甄偉成、劉華、劉濤、王玉華、劉士軍、劉輝、曹世明、譚家衛、何小芝、譚琳、曹詩朋、曹詩羽、劉德萍、于小冉、于連陞、姜明澔、白家毓、許德明、常言芳、王曉林、王爲民、李倩倩、王若般、王小文、王爲勝、王若冰、王賽菊、鄭國懷、李衛清、鄭舒文、陳代明、陸雪梅、陳子安、謝小雁、謝小雁的寶寶、金胤、原守順、賀長江、宋海天、胡慶輝、徐晶、賈虎、孫悅洋、張偉國、王天鎮、王榮珍、丁愛榮、孫永山、包桂芝、趙鳳珍、劉福愚、劉寧、劉淑華、劉淑惠、李曉君、常君、孟慶君、常建奧、董須賢、朱珊珊、朱成勇、陳素平、朱弘昊、顏兆波、江奇渝、故陳碧英、安臻、劉彩雲、劉彩琴、劉占士、劉芳、劉麗娜、傘吉碩、傘俊博、傘洪飛、陳艷波、溫榮錦、鄭德義、鄭爽、馬濤、祁雅平、么作榮、李安平、周家太、周建超、何淑芹、故董恩波、曹秋芳、楊玉霞、張遠濤、陳淑雲、胡聆玉、劉建新、馬德璞、周桂霞、陳幼祥、謝夏芬、馬剛、陳慧苓、馬天慧、馬天宇、蔡澤平、蔡思宇、丁效坤、邢本明、李淑繁、趙欣慰、侯麗萍、王雯紅、邢蘊、故邢普鐸、王國山、王紅霞(吉林)、王弘巖、王自南、張玲　96元：故謝少紅　92元：陳潔　70元：席寶莉、師璐、師耀先　66元：傅明權、劉星資　64元：隱名氏　60元：汪小芝　58元：朱存、朱建美、韓紅妹、楊成荷、楊宇　50元：于美魯、劉祥瑾、廖漢卿、陳登梅、李世木、故姜陳氏、楊紅英、姚炳山、陳敏道、陳雅娟、歐駛瑋、宋帆、盧慶杰、王靜(流通處)、鄭建盛、陳濤、陸銀寶、李燕紅、呂雙雲、朱士安、王和順、蔡儷、謝一峰、魏鳳林、王書靜、林長江、林福榮、李小紅、隱名氏、王桂芝(瀋陽)、故韓明、殷斌、郭一鳴、陳臻、胡佳卉、陳文偉、張慧珠、胡信昌、李慧霞　40元：皺積善、善忠清、孫鴻、皺鳳、孫同浩、鄭賀祥　38元：劉冬培　35元：何玉梅、鄧翔宇　30元：譚仕英　25元：故姜殿清、故王玉珍、姜國華、袁秀勤、袁愛華、王施媛、遲震霖　20元：席志明、韓秀琴、王琳琳、故殷謁多、故張氏、故殷日明、故袁明、故譚凌雲、故袁鳳信、殷日紅、宋國清　18元：故朱德祥、故李秀英、故韓汝山、故萬肖冬　15元：王彩琴、殷武義、殷海榕、殷國義、隱名氏　10元：韓玉華、董華、李治道、李虹然、董艷、孫續桂、孫蓮芝　5元：董德文、李學玲、董凱明

美金部份：（US$）

4000元：Te Hsiu Chang　900元：蘇清江　180元：李君唐、陸桂玉　100元：朱欽　90元：葉潔薇、黃亦明、曹淑澔、孫紅梅、孫培起、蘇振英、李威儒、許湘靈、李進益、吳宛儒、吳嘉恭、吳淑禎、吳卓儒、藍哲儒、藍豔燦、林素惠、吳佳眞、吳月女、吳天生、吳學熙、邱珵輝、楊蘭、吳美瑩、何林鈞、林斌、陳永瑞、邵千純、陳雯萱、陳怡仲、陳怡寧、邵豐吉、邵陳世玉、雷洪健、湯麗明、雷炎榮、雷嘉茵、施秀珍、郭子琪、陳遠碩、陳慧玲、唐永念、盧麗鴻、李振道、唐永良、盧麗賢

隨喜助印名單

台幣部分：（NT$）（若指定僅助印七書中某經者，即含在此項中）

(一)大日經疏：林金興(9000元)、李宜倫(5000元)，林寶惠(4000元)，釋玄定、袁炳亨、邱淑琴(各2000元)，翁祥瀕、劉芳潔、陳俊忠、黃慧儀(各1000元)，劉佳蓁(800元)，廖世民(600元)，林文哲、黃吉豐、郭俊麟(各500元)，周麗雲(300元)，林財慶、林枝富、簡秀夏(各200元)。　(二)大乘百法明門論今註：故程英(10000元)，楊志賢(300元)。

美金部份：（US$）　（2015.4.11止）

林楊秀英($4000)，Da Ray Trading Company($600)，蔡興邦($344)，蔡維德、蔡維瑞、蔡

維行、邱溪鶴、邱盧秀菊、邱玉枝、方瑞娥、邱美玲(各$314)，鄭和興($200)，林瑞惠($160)，故圓平、邱育葦、邱昱斌(各$72)，David Meade($70)，金祥運、故唐定坤、故劉定燕、故盧萬全、故李鳳安、故盧麗霞、故盧熙宜、故黃用小、故盧松、故盧順、故余振邦、故李杏(各$20)，李威儒、范小紅、范文娟、陸銀寶、薛根娣、周建新、周婷、周安娜、Alden Walker(各$10)

「毘盧印經會」基本會員名單

台幣部分：

釋成觀、釋信覺、釋傳藏、釋眞際、釋慧芸、釋見拓、釋眞願、林秀英、張淑鈴、李錫昌、李陳紫、李淑媛、李宗憲、陳慧貞、李淑瑩、李怡欣、李啓揚、張大政、張金員、蕭惠玲、吳蕭幼、宮林玉蘭、宮貴英、宮桂華、吳龍海、蘇金滿、張進財、趙文璋、張正昌、廖世宏、王韻蕙、鄭惠貞、藍翊豪、藍進士、藍秀鳳、藍謝有親、藍翊瑋、藍玉玲、藍宜建、藍順、藍偉誠、藍宜助、何啓政、謝邦珍、丘聿台、劉芊瑩、丘祖毅、黃淑玉、梁震亞、劉慧玲、莊振臺、劉千維、楊錦芳、蘇進培、蘇詠筑、蕭敏璋、林秀芬、李盈瑩、故林蕭玉盎、林育生、鐘暉雅、林弘彬、林伊璇、林育禾、歐梅如、蘇盈潔、張菁樺、林滄敏、林雁萱、林雁萱、林筠、林佩慧、楊三品、楊婕妤、楊盛博、林佩瑤、楊子孟、楊承熹、楊承學、楊振聰、故楊李雪花、顏珮娜、馮翰琦、林桂芳、陳姬、施秉宏、沈蕙敏、王素禎、林麗貞、沈蒼元、郭冠廷、吳政霖、吳政儒、朱嘉惠、林志欣、萬靄雲、林燦璋、陳彤曲、許雅惠、廖偉成。

人民幣部分：

釋成觀、釋眞體、釋眞明、林益謙、李萍、蔣曉峰、李琴梅、彭翠、鮑羚、苗欣雨、唐雅琴、衣麗萍、魏玉鳳、陳桂榮、陳泓羽、陳艷波、李華(北京)、朱存、李娟、孫貴福、王淑芬、孔曉峰、戴韻秋、陳健、吳彬、陳一銘、仇笑梅、黃福生、于文君、宋惠林、宋瑜、趙晟景、王焉勝、朱立春、肖惠銖、陶宇紅、馬增奇、秦文韜、秦爽、王清芬、秦士興、劉榮煥、馬一鈞、黃愛萍、袁維孝、師義、覃亞文、李霞、覃曉菲、冼玉琪、柳文梅、陳艷、丁新林、丁照龍、田偉、王萍、孫艷、李遠靜、張淑德、曹勇、李華(蘇州)、鄭斯月、王賽菊、王賽眞、陳臻、陳碧如、沈金蓮、宋亞莉、蘇展、呂捷、鄭錦娥、蒲瑞英、張智博、王宛巖、張紅偉、張沃明、孫艷立、魯靜、呂文秀、林建兵、裘彬、吳域、王宏敏、隱名氏、周瑞蘭、王海鉗、高玉、王自南、丁豹祥、王猛輝、胡紅杰、故馬興正、李文奇、孫彩華、朱延民、故福田、王輝、李海青、苗虹、聞睿、杜洋、徐程、鐘雅哲、董廷方、劉祥瑾、趙錫期、趙美容、鄭雪雲、常君、田桂珍、郝麗威、李淑華、王超、許涵、韓永紅、孟慶玲、周淑敏、孫建茹、安臻、劉淑華、陳榕錦、劉玲、孟保臣、韋佳、趙永群、陳克流、陳自強、李靈均、王曉葉、許小片、朱穀、徐小丹、劉宇、章賦。

「遍照印經會」基本會員名單

釋成觀、釋信覺、吳曉、簡慶惠、陳衍隆、陳遠碩、陳慧玲、邵豐吉、邵陳世玉、陳永瑞、邵千純、陳雯萱、陳怡仲、陳怡寧、唐永念、陳國輝、吳秀芬、葉潔薇、邵俊雄、李應華、林斌、蘇清江、唐永良、詹朱界宗、LaVern Dean Loomis、詹雅如、嚴愛民、何林鈞、李宗勳、許碧鳳、李安怡、李郁芬、陳淑瑜、謝幸貞、劉嘉仁、黃育英、劉慧上、劉圓眞、盧麗鴻、劉文娜、盧麗賢、何方、吳宛儒、吳朝暉、陶姍姍、高斐、吳厚萱、吳美萱、Patricia Litkowski

修　盡　悉　若　下　上　莊　願
行　於　發　有　濟　報　嚴　以
無　未　菩　見　三　四　佛　此
上　來　提　聞　塗　重　淨　功
道　際　心　者　苦　恩　土　德

回
向
偈

禪之甘露（英文版）
THE SWEET DEWS OF CH'AN

作　者：釋成觀法師
倡印者：大毘盧寺(台灣)・遍照寺(美國)
出版者：新逍遙園譯經院
贈送處：台灣：新逍遙園譯經院、大毘盧寺
　　　　台北市11691文山區福興路4巷6弄15號
　　　　Tel：(02)2934-7281・Fax：(02)2930-1919
　　　　美國：遍照寺Americana Buddhist Temple
　　　　10515 N. Latson Rd., Howell, MI 48855, USA
　　　　Tel: (517)545-7559・Fax: (517)545-7558
贊助專戶：(1)華南銀行公館分行
　　　　　帳號：118-20-090652-0　戶名：釋成觀
　　　　　(2)郵政劃撥帳號：15126341　戶名：釋成觀
免費下載網址：www.abtemple.org
承印者：東豪印刷事業有限公司
版　次：佛曆2559年(2015年5月)釋迦牟尼佛聖誕四版四刷
　　　　敬印二千冊(本書含在此次倡印之七書中)
國際書碼：ISBN 957-9373-15-9

南無護法韋馱尊天菩薩

Namo Wei-to Pusa, the Honorable Celestial Guardian of Mahayana